FITTING & SHOWING THE
HALTER HORSE

PRENTICE
HALL PRESS
EQUESTRIAN
BOOKS

FITTING & SHOWING THE HALTER HORSE

LYNDA BLOOM

PRENTICE HALL PRESS
New York London Toronto Sydney Tokyo

Published in 1987 by Prentice Hall Press
A Division of Simon & Schuster, Inc.
Gulf + Western Building
One Gulf + Western Plaza
New York, NY 10023

Originally published by Arco Publishing, Inc.

PRENTICE HALL PRESS is a trademark of Simon & Schuster, Inc.

Library of Congress Cataloging-in-Publication Data

Bloom, Lynda.
  Fitting and showing the halter horse.
  Includes index.
  1. Horse-shows—Halter classes.   2.   Horses—Showing.
I.   Title.
SF296.H34B56   636.1′08′88   79-13615
ISBN 0-668-04431-4

Manufactured in the United States of America

10 9 8 7 6 5 4

For the countless halter winners they have led, and
for always being there when I needed them,
this book is dedicated to
Tom and Brenda Long

1   BREEDING

2   SELECTION

3   FORMATION

4   TRAINING

5   CARE OF TRAINING

6   EXERCISE

7   WORK

8

9   OBTAINING

10 MANAGE

11 DISEASE

12 SHOWING

Index

Contents

1   BREEDING FOR HALTER WINNERS   1

2   SELECTING A HALTER PROSPECT   16

3   FORMULATING FEED AND WORMING PROGRAMS   31

4   TRAINING THE HALTER HORSE   44

5   CARE OF THE FEET AND LEGS   67

6   EXERCISE—THE KEY TO FITNESS   79

7   WORKING ON PROBLEM AREAS   96

8   COAT CARE AND GROOMING   109

9   CLIPPING AND TRIMMING THE HALTER HORSE   128

10   MANES AND TAILS   160

11   DRESSING THE HALTER HORSE   177

12   SHOWING THE HALTER HORSE   194

    INDEX   213

Chapter 1

Breeding for Halter Winners

Heroes are born, not made. Breeding for halter horses is a risky business, but it still keeps us plugging away, trying time after time to produce that colt or filly that is going to "win the world."

Possibly you're a mare owner who is thinking about raising some halter prospects. Or maybe you don't own a mare now, but you are looking for one. To limit the element of breeding risk, it's wise to select the best broodmare you can find, and take it to the best stud. Why?

Dr. J. Warren Evans, of the Department of Animal Science, University of California in Davis, is one of the nation's leading educators and research specialists in the field of equine physiology. At the 1978 California Livestock Symposium in Fresno, he spoke to an audience of horsemen on the subject of making the decision of whether or not to breed a certain mare. He quickly found that money hits close to home. By the time Dr. Evans had completed a look at breeding economics, the breeders and prospective breeders who listened to his speech were getting wiser. They were having second thoughts about breeding mares that weren't "up to par."

1

To minimize the risks of breeding, choose the best mare you can. This classy duo is from the Whalen Ranch, Gilroy, California.

THE ECONOMICS OF BREEDING

While outlining the costs involved, Dr. Evans made the astounding statement that everything has to "double" because a breeder just can't plan on getting a marketable foal from a mare each and every year. The question asked most often is, How long does a breeder have to keep a mare to get a good foal? Dr. Evans explained. "If you start thinking about the current conception percentage, we're dealing with roughly an 80 per cent conception rate for mares in general. If these 80 out of 100 mares do conceive, only about 90 per cent of those will have a live foal. So, we have about a 72 per cent chance of getting a live, healthy foal. Only about 70 per cent of *these* foals are going to be marketable, or will have a useful purpose because of problems after foaling such as death, injury or illness, and there is also a 'poor quality' factor."

Because of these circumstances, Dr. Evans made it clear, a breeder can count on getting a good marketable foal from his mare only about once every *two* years. For this reason, costs are effectively "doubled."

The cost of keeping a mare over that two-year period vary, depending on whether or not the mare is kept at home. Some owners are forced to board their horses. Feed costs naturally vary from place to place, as do veterinarian fees. Start adding things up. Feed alone, if you give the mare only alfalfa each day, will come to about $300 a year. Then, if you don't keep the mare at home, you'll have to include the board costs. You'll also have bills from your farrier, vet costs, and then the breeding expenses. First, there's the booking fee, then the costs of hauling the mare to the stallion, the board while she's there (which could well be $5.50 per day or higher). There are vet expenses for culturing and pregnancy checks. The stud fee is generally payable before the mare leaves the stallion station. Dr. Evans added up these costs, figuring the one-foal-every-two-years factor and threw out a ballpark figure giving the symposium audience an idea of what that one, good marketable foal would cost. The day the little fellow hits the ground, you will likely have $3,832 invested in those wobbly legs, that bony body and that adorable face. And, for the sake of that nearly "four grand," he'd better be more than *cute* when he grows up.

Don't throw in the towel. The information above is not aimed at discouraging you from breeding your own halter prospects. The purpose of the preceding is to open your eyes to the investment that a horse really is, and to make you aware that selective breeding is the key to show ring success—and the pass key to that high rise penthouse that stands high above, and throws a shadow on, the Poor House.

SELECTING FOR BREEDING

Successful breeders work hard at lowering the risks involved in breeding. The best way to do that is to start with a top-notch

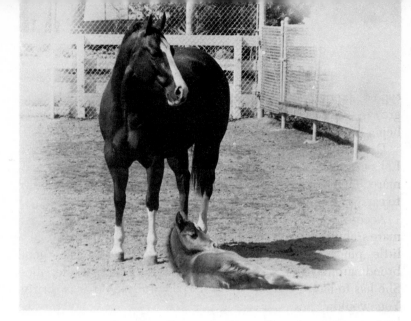

A foal is a big investment. Lightning Lady, a broodmare at the Whalen Ranch, was selected because of her top quality and ability to produce a "good investment."

mare—the best one you can find. If you don't know exactly what to look for in a mare, ask for help. Successful halter horse breeders will be happy to show you their mares and tell you what they like in a broodmare. A good veterinarian can also guide you in trying to breed for a winner. He'll look at it on the basis of what characteristics a mare needs to be capable of carrying a foal and being a good mother, and what hereditary traits a mare might have or lack that could help or hinder getting a good foal.

Jim Burns, D.V.M., from Sunol, California, has been specializing in the problems of broodmares for a number of years. He's also been the broodmare vet at one of California's leading Thoroughbred breeding operations. He often finds parallels between what he'd like to see in a halter broodmare, and what breeders look for in trying to produce running horses. Both type of produce will be "performing" at early ages, need early growth and, of course, need the potential to do what they're being bred for.

Dr. Burns always cautions breeders on the element of risk. Let's examine, first, what makes a mare a good risk as a broodmare, not particularly as a halter producer, but just in her ability to carry and raise a good foal.

According to Dr. Burns, depth of body is important in a mare's ability to carry a foal. "You wouldn't want to breed a little, pinched-up mare. A mare that's destined to be a good broodmare has to have some appealing physical characteristics. She has to have *balance*. She has to be of a type that is thrifty. You wouldn't want to use a mare that tends to stay far too lean, or is too nervous.

"You want a mare that's feminine and motherly. This, you can only find out by trial and error. The motherly characteristics are those of kindness, and this is important as the environment of the baby foal dictates a lot about his mental attitude as he grows up. You don't want a real cranky mare that's going to raise a foal that's going to be a crank. Again, it's trial and error. You have to watch a mare in action during the period of time she takes to raise a foal, which would be on the average of four to six months."

So, look for a well-balanced mare with good depth, a good deep barrel and one that is well sprung in the hips and chest. And, especially when breeding for halter horses, Dr. Burns says, "You need a mare that has appealing characteristics overall, because when you're looking to cut the risk, you can hardly expect an extremely ugly mare to raise a pretty baby. They'll occasionally do it, but it goes on the law of averages. You can't often get a silk purse out of a sow's ear."

Looking at the photo of the black and white Paint mare Amigo Babe (incidentally, a top producer), Dr. Burns commented, "This mare is nice and deep through the barrel, has a good, long bottom line, and has a fine, well sprung hip." All

*Amigo Babe, owned by Duke Neff, Peculiar, Missouri, is the pro-
ducer of two National Champions and two APHA Champions. She
possesses conformation features that point to her ability to easily
carry a foal.*

of these things help in a mare's ability to carry a foal. Amigo
is also pretty, and feminine class is important in a broodmare.

Dr. Burns says to, "Take a broodmare, a good broodmare, as
one that would be capable of producing the most desirable offspring . . . those which would be left after natural selection
weeded out the others. This you find sometimes through trial
and error, but you try to use all of your natural instincts plus
good, common sense. You can't do it by simply reading a pedigree."

"A pedigree won't tell you or show you what a mare can
produce, or whether or not she'll be a good broodmare. A pedigree *can* tell you if there is desirable blood up close in the
pedigree. The farther back the good blood, the less desirable
it is. Six generations back is blood that's pretty well diluted."

Judge the *individual.* When you're breeding for halter horses,
you do have to pay more attention to your mare. An ugly mare
would not be likely to produce a classic halter horse. And, by
the same token, in the Thoroughbred breeding business where

records of money earned are used to dictate how breedings are arranged, you would never expect a mare to produce a foal that would earn more money than the best earner in the first four generations of her pedigree. The blood *does* have to be there, but you have to look closely at the individual, rather than just the pedigree. Says Dr. Burns, "The pedigree simply guides you as to what you could *expect* that mare to produce, but the mare herself shows you the actual truth when she produces, good or bad."

Be sure to avoid hereditary traits in broodmares which could lead to undesirable foals. For halter horses, you especially need to be careful to get straight legs, properly set knees and hocks, good top and bottom lines, classic heads and necks. You must pay attention to detail. You don't take a mare that toes out, breed her to a stallion that toes in, and expect to get a foal that is "right square in the center." You might get a foal that has one foot pointing in and one pointing out! This is more joke than fact; but if you breed two problem horses, you can expect heredity to give you one or more of the problems in the foal.

Another problem is parrot mouth. Many judges check for it in halter classes, especially in the mare and stallion classes. A badly parrot mouthed horse has difficulty eating. Some can't even graze, because they can't bite off the grass. More than just an eating problem, however, Dr. Burns warns against this undesirable trait. "The genetic characteristic that goes with parrot mouth may offer you more faults than just the parrot mouth alone. If something is shrunken about the head, what's to say that the rest of the head should be normal? For instance, the size of the brain or the circulation in the brain can be abnormal, which would dictate whether or not you had an intelligent animal. Parrot mouth is definitely an undesirable characteristic in a broodmare and also in a stallion."

One of the advantages of being a mare owner is the sea of material on available stallions you can look over and compare when you're looking to breed your mare. You can examine the show records of a stallion's foals, see photos of these winners and, by screening the advertising, spot the producers of big winners to help you decide which horses you should seriously consider. Then, talk to the breeders, go see the foals, look at the get of the stallions in the halter classes at a show.

You don't always stop here, because there are other considerations. Dr. Burns says that, "Some stallions get early maturing horses. You can spot this tendency in the regular X-ray. In the epiphyseal closure in yearlings, you'll find that some stallions produce yearlings that close early, some that close late. This will tip you off as to early or late maturity. It depends on what you are looking for: how important maturity rate is to you. If you're after a nice cutting horse prospect that will be six years old before he's working hard, you don't care if a colt matures early. With a halter horse, you definitely want him maturing early. That's the sum total of your goal at that point.

"However, if you're a purist about breeding horses, you have to look *beyond* two-year-old halter classes. You want a horse that can go on from there and do things. It makes you wonder why many two-year-old halter champions never go beyond, or develop, to any more. Bone soundness is the big factor. Maybe a horse is really cute when he's a baby, or a two-year-old, but after that he develops unsoundness characteristics because of genetic weakness in the bone structure. You have to wonder why these horses are judged high at halter. Maybe that's just what the breed is looking for at the time . . . a 'picture horse' that can't do anything."

This statement brings up the "halter horse versus performance horse" argument, which you'll find discussed in the next chapter. But Dr. Burns doesn't mean to infer that there's something wrong with all halter horses or the judges who judge them. What he is concerned about is that certain things are considered "attractive" on a halter horse that really shouldn't be thought of in that manner. One such feature, dainty feet, seems to be a fad with halter horses. Dr. Burns says to watch out!

"When breeding, you *should* worry about the size of the foot. In halter classification, they seem to want a really small footed animal. A tiny footed animal, however, is one that might have foot problems later on. You have to be wary about that type of thing. You should seek out a nice, well developed foot, with a good, deep wall and plenty of square inches to the area of the foot itself. This is especially true when you're packing a massive, well muscled horse on little, tiny feet. There are more pounds and pressure per square inch of foot and more chance of problems later on."

When to Breed

How about the age of the broodmare? Luckily, if you have a mare that has foaled two or three times, you can observe what she's capable of having. This probably puts her in an average age category. But, what about breeding a young mare? Dr. Burns feels that breeding a three-year-old is acceptable, *if* the mare tends to grow fast, is mature for her age and is in top health. A small, immature, three-year-old would possibly have the remainder of her growth and maturity somewhat arrested by being bred at this age.

You'll see many mares producing well into their twenties. Healthy reproductive systems are essential for raising good foals. Dr. Burns suggests that breeders simply remember that, "A twenty year old mare has twenty year old uterine lining with twenty year old ovaries that have ruptured and bled every twenty-one days for nineteen years." The ability to go on producing in the twenties is strictly an individual ability that varies from mare to mare.

It seems all of us are breeding for the halter prospect that arrives sixty seconds after the New Year's Eve party really comes alive. That January first foal is just "that much ahead" of the other ones. Trying to get a mare to cycle properly for a breeding to produce an early foal is a problem, because the mare's normal cycle to breed is April through August. Dr. Burns says, "Maybe the problem is not breeding mares in January, but in the standards of arbitrary judging we have selected for the offspring."

While some halter futurities have breakdowns for the weanlings, judging early foals against those of the same, and late foals against other late foals, *most* judging is still based on the "January first syndrome," so the problem exists of trying to convince a mare that she's to be bred in January or February. "If a mare *must* be bred this early," says Dr. Burns, "there are ways of imposing an artificial season. Infrared light programs are used. Occasionally, a thyroid supplement helps, and there is a chemical called Prostaglandin which may help some mares." Rely on your veterinarian for advice.

BREEDING FOR COLOR

Waiting close to a year for a foal to hit the ground is agonizing enough, but add to this the perils of the color breeder and you see the increase in risk. But, it must all be worth it, or so many breeders wouldn't be involved in it. When you're trying for a Paint, Pinto or Appaloosa foal, you can reduce the risk of a solid foal somewhat by your mare selection. While Dr. Burns spoke of selecting the individual rather than just reading pedigrees, he was clear to note that some indications of what a mare *should* be capable of producing *are* shown in the pedigree. With color, this is often the case. For instance, in going to the cross of colored horse on an American Quarter Horse Association (AQHA) registered mare, you'll find certain bloodlines of AQHA pedigrees are more prone to produce colored foals.

In Iowa Park, Texas, at the 2J Horse Farm, the Stanley Williamsons, and their son, Joe, have been producing top Paint horses for years. They stand on top in the All Time Leading Breeders of Paint Halter Horses in the American Paint Horse

Rodeo Cowboy, pictured at ten weeks of age, became a halter winner at open and Paint shows. His dam is an AQHA mare, sired by a son of Leo Tag. The "Leo" line of horses are good color producers. This foal's dam produced three Paint foals in a row, when bred to the Paint stud, Painted Shoshone.

Association standings. Their Supreme Champion stallion, Yellow Mount, has been topping the lists as a halter and performance sire for many years. The dun and white stallion is, at this writing, the nation's leading Paint sire. His own show records attest for "like breeds like." His Supreme Championship was the first one awarded after the American Pinto Horse Association ruling to include success at the rack track as one of the requirements. He's been a halter and performance national champion and is no doubt the best known Paint horse in the industry.

Joe Williamson feels that choosing the right mare to go to a stallion like this is a definite advantage in increasing the chances of getting a Paint foal. Most of the mares at the 2J Ranch now, there to be bred to Yellow Mount and another stallion, Top Yellow, are AQHA mares with close-up breeding to Bright Bars and Bright Eyes. They have mares who, through Stage Hand, go to Skipper W., and also some Leo mares. These bloodlines all represent breeding which produces a great deal of white. By using mares of this type, the Williamsons can feel a little more certain of their chances of getting Paint foals.

Because a mare doesn't have a colored foal one year doesn't mean she won't sport a Paint foal the next time around. Joe doesn't give up. He cited one mare which had four solid foals in a row, then presented them with the best Paint colt ever born on the place. Perseverence is often the key.

Also in the Williamson's breeding program are several mares registered in the Paint Breeding Stock Registry. These are mares with one or both Paint parents, yet the mares did not have sufficient color to qualify them for regular registry. Because the 2J breeds so many overo Paints, if they do get a solid filly, they have to consider the fact that she may be carrying the color gene. Research shows that even though the overo coat pattern isn't present, the gene can still be carried. This is why the mating of two AQHA registered horses often produces an excessive white colt, or a Paint "crop out" . . . the color genes are sneaking in from the past. Quite the opposite, however, is the Paint tobiano pattern. In order for a horse to carry the tobiano gene, the color must be present on the coat.

Breeding for Appaloosas is another area where the color risk can be narrowed by proper mare selection. There's no guarantee, but the risk seems smaller if you choose mares that come from strains known to produce color.

Halcyon Farms in Morgan Hill, California, is the home for the Appaloosa stallion, Bright Chip, who has, since 1970, either been the state's leading sire, or runner-up. Bright Chip has produced an endless list of halter winners, including a United States National Champion and a World Champion. This top color and conformation producer is a son of Bright Eyes Brother.

Since Eugene and Doris Sharp, owners of Halcyon Farms, purchased Bright Chip, they've had an amazing color percent-

In breeding for Appaloosas, mare selection can help reduce the chances of a solid foal. This is a Robin Reed bred AQHA mare, with her suckling son of the Appaloosa stallion, Bright Chip.

age record on his foals. In the stallion's lifetime, he's sired over 400 foals, all either foaled with color, or coloring very shortly after. Because of the stallion's incredible ability to produce spotted foals, the Sharps don't have to be that worried about narrowing the color risk, but they'll be the first to tell you that it never hurt anyone to choose mares capable of producing color. They have Leo bred mares, Bright Bar and Robin Reed mares in their pastures. The Sharps would definitely suggest that breeders look for mares such as these when they are breeding for color.

On the pastures of Halcyon Farms, AQHA and Thoroughbred mares graze with their foals . . . a 100 per cent color crop.

An Appaloosa-to-Appaloosa cross produced this bay and white son
of Bright Chip, out of the top show mare, Capay Miss Chips.

Chapter 2

Selecting a Halter Prospect

The way to win at halter is to pick a top horse, then make him look even better through proper conditioning. You certainly can't take a poor horse and move him up the ladder simply because his coat shines. You start with the best, and it keeps you on top.

Eye on the Champions

A look at some of the nation's most outstanding halter horses will give you an idea of what judges are looking for. Take a look at the photograph of the AQHA stallion, Skipa Star. Once a World Champion Two Year Old Halter Champion, he is thought of by many to be the most perfectly conformed horse ever to enter the halter ring. At major shows, during twenty-eight months of campaigning, Skipa Star won every one of the 56 halter classes in which he was shown. He stood Grand Champion 44 times, Reserve Grand 10 times. Standing at the Wilson Ranch in Pattison, Texas, Skipa Star is a son of Skipper's Lad, by Skipper W.

And, how about Ricky Bonanza? Another AQHA stallion, he is the world's leading, living, point-earning halter stallion. A son of Coy's Bonanza, he has 374 AQHA halter points, 138 Grand Championships, 36 Reserve Championships and won 98 straight firsts at halter in a 98 show series.

Skipa Star, thought by many to be the most perfect halter horse ever shown. Photo by Darol Dickinson.

The world's leading living point-earning halter stallion, Ricky Bonanza.

Paul F Bar, also an AQHA stallion, is also shown in Palomino classes. He has been World Champion Palomino Halter and Color Horse. In one year of campaigning in Palomino shows, he had over 55 Grand and Reserve Championships. In two years of AQHA halter classes, he won 48 Grands and Reserves and qualified for the AQHA World Championship Show. Paul F Bar is owned by Windy Hill Ranch in Waynesboro, Georgia.

In Gilroy, California, at the ranch of John and Sandy Ballard, an AQHA stallion resides in the "King's Suite." Sugar Wes, an AQHA Champion, is also an AQHA Superior Halter Horse, with over 100 halter points. The Ballards are breeders of Quarter Horses, but not professional trainers. Through the selection of the *right* horse, and diligence in fitting and showing him, they have taken this horse to his many titles without the help of a professional trainer. This fine halter horse also has points earned in Western Pleasure, Working Cowhorse, Steer Roping and

Paul F Bar, many times champion at AQHA and Palomino shows.

Sugar Wes, AQHA Champion and Superior Halter Horse, owned by Ballard's Quarter Horses, Gilroy, California.

Champions produce champions. Wendy Ann Wes, daughter of Sugar Wes, won two weanling halter futurities in 1978.

Western Riding. In 1978, he was Junior Working Cowhorse Champion for the Pacific Coast Quarter Horse Association. For those who profess that halter horses can only stand and "look pretty" and not perform, Sugar Wes has many people eating crow.

Al Anderson, a halter horse trainer from Wilton, California, showed the Appaloosa stallion, Dart's Le Bar, in Oklahoma City in 1977 to win the title of World's Champion Two Year Old Appaloosa Halter Stallion. This horse is owned by John Gonigan, and is still being campaigned by Anderson. Again, the

1977 World's Champion Two Year Old Appaloosa Stallion, Dart's Le Bar.

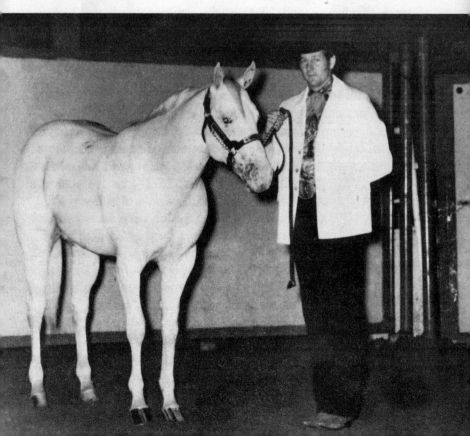

right horse was chosen and a talented person fit him correctly and took him to the winner's circle.

What do all these champions have in common? Naturally, they have superior conformation, but tied in with that is the key word—BALANCE. They are beautifully put together, balanced, and they represent the ideals of their breed standards. This book is concerned with the Western-type horse. Whether it be a Quarter Horse, an Appaloosa, a Paint, a Palomino, or a stock-type Pinto, we are basically striving for the conformation standard of the Quarter Horse.

WHAT JUDGES LOOK FOR

Years ago, the standard was for the small horse, standing not more than 14.2 hands. Today, the modern day halter horse is larger and bolder, and because of the infusion of Thoroughbred blood into the Quarter Horse, a great deal more size is complemented by breediness and long muscle. The horse is no longer the "bulldog" type, or a "chunk." Today's halter horse needs definite muscle, but not too much, when you compare him to days gone by.

There will always be that controversy over whether or not a halter horse can make a performance horse. The real horsemen, who are judging halter classes today, *are* oriented to a horse that is not only capable of doing something, but also capable of holding up and remaining sound through hard use. A balanced, correct horse will do just that.

When you're looking for balance, the best way to view a halter horse is in thirds. Stand back from him and view him first as an overall individual. Then, divide him visually into three parts, from the head to the back of the shoulder, then to the flank, and from the flank to the back of the hip. Do all three parts complement each other? Do they tie in well with each other? A horse with a very long body but a short stubby neck and short hip is not balanced. A large head on the end of a long, thin neck makes you wonder if this imbalance will cause the horse to drown in his water tub! Everything must fit, with all the parts blending and none looking out of place.

The ideal halter horse has a head so pretty you can't take your eyes off it! It should be a head with lots of expression. The forehead should be flat, the ears short and pert, and the muzzle fine and refined. This should all be enhanced by big, kind eyes.

A great deal of emphasis today is put on the throatlatch, and rightly so. A horse with a fine, small throatlatch will be more able to drop his nose and bridle well when he's ridden. Judges who have ridden performance horses will be especially aware of the type of throatlatch and neck your horse has. Breeders have been striving over the past few years to greatly improve the throatlatches and necks on their horses and they truly have modernized them.

The neck of the halter horse should be thin and long and set fairly high on the shoulders. The prettiest necks seem to be the ones with a very subtle arc from the withers to the poll. This is not in any way a crest, but just a very pretty shape to the neck. A neck that is set low in the shoulders and is flat on top is not desirable.

The shoulder of a halter horse should lay back well, and if you're lucky, the slope of the shoulder will match that of your horse's pastern. A horse with a good, sloping shoulder is a better, more free-moving horse that can reach with his front end and move with ease, not bouncing and chopping with each step. This type of horse is nicer to ride and also has a better chance of staying sound.

Withers should be well defined. Mutton withered horses don't hold saddles well, and any judge who has ever ridden one is certain to avoid them when he thinks about placing his halter class. The judge is also looking at the top line of the horse. This should be level, for if the withers are lower than the croup it results in a horse who travels very heavily on his front end.

Keep in mind that young horses grow up in back until the front catches up. Very often, during their growth, the hip is much higher than the withers, but what you hope for at the big finish is a horse with a level top line.

A deep heart girth is an asset on a halter horse, as long as it balances with the rest of the body. The horse that is big and deep in the front end, but has very little hip, is not balanced. A deep horse that is very shortlegged is not balanced. Ideally, if you measured the heart girth on a balanced horse, you would find it was the same distance as the measurement from the belly to the ground.

A horse with a good, long hip truly stands out in today's halter classes. Why? The horse's ability to move well and perform is greatly centered around that hip and the strength and impulsion the hip can give. When looking at the hip, look at the distance from the flank to the back of the hip for the depth, and the length of the hip from its start under the tail set to how far it drops to tie-in above the gaskin area. It should be deep and long, and when a horse like this receives proper fitting, the muscle tone accentuates the length and depth and you have a truly impressive hip.

Moving down from the hip, we judge the gaskins. This is another area that is strongly criticized by judges. Many horses have a lot of muscle on the outside of the gaskin, but little on the inside. If you want to check for balance and correctness, you would draw a visual line straight down the tendon of the back of the upper hind leg. You would find half the gaskin on each side of the line, with equal amounts of inside and outside muscle.

When judging, a judge will look hard at the hocks of a halter horse. They should, when viewed from the side, fall in a line directly under the horse's tail set. If the hocks are too far under, the horse is sickle hocked. If they stick out too far behind, this is also a fault. Again, the judges are looking for an ability to perform, and correctness to insure soundness.

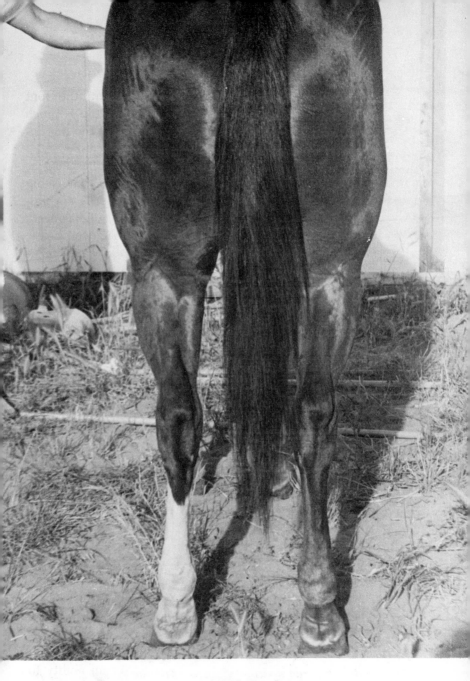

A good back leg is an asset to any halter horse.

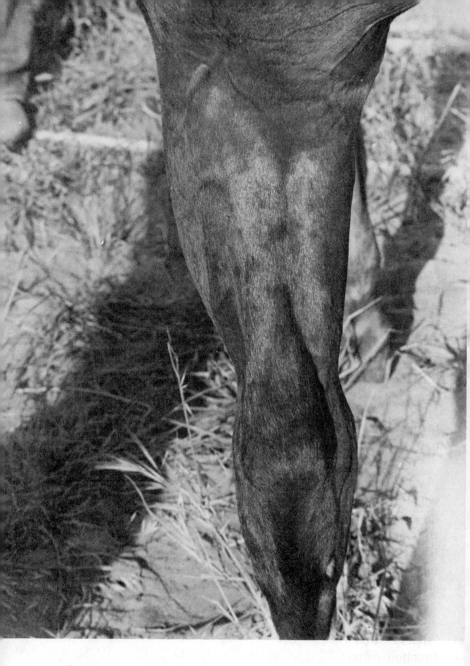

The amount of inside and outside muscle on the gaskin should be equal.

If you were to stand behind a horse and view his back legs, you would want them to come directly down. Bow legs are not acceptable. Cow hocks, where the hocks turn in, are another fault, as are hocks that stick out to the side. You should be able to drop a plumb line and have that leg look straight and true.

Front legs are looked at, by many judges, more than most other parts of the body. Two-thirds of a horse's weight is carried by his front legs, and if they are not true and correct, the weight will eventually break them down. It's as simple as that.

Looking from the side, a halter horse should have a short cannon bone. The forearm should be longer than the cannon. This is not only structurally sound, but it is the sign of a potential athlete. Performance trainers feel the closer the knees and hocks are to the ground, the handier a horse will be.

The forearm and cannon are, naturally, tied together by the knee. The cannon should extend directly from the bottom of the knee, when looking from the side. The knee should not bend back (called a calf knee), or go forward (over at the knee). Both are faults, but the calf kneed horse is more likely to become unsound than the horse who is over at the knee. If the horse is correct, soundness problems are minimized.

Looking from the front, the plumb line again comes into play. When the cannon bone drops from the knee, it should come out dead center. There should be equal amount of knee on each side of the top of the cannon bone. If a knee is offset, the cannon comes out more on one side than the other, and strain is put on the inside or the outside of the cannon bone, depending on which way the knee is offset. This is often a cause of splints.

The shoulders and pasterns of a horse should have the same good angle and slope. They act as shock absorbers. If the "shocks" aren't made to do the work, the "machine" doesn't function correctly. The result? Possible unsoundness. This is why you look for a horse who slopes well, and does not have short, straight-up-and-down pasterns. He'll stay sound longer and will certainly be a better mover.

You may wonder why judges will place one horse low if it has a splint and place another horse higher even though it also has splints. What are they looking for? Basically, the cause of splints are varied and a judge will look for the *reason* for the splint. If a horse is incorrect in the legs, and splints have been caused by this fault, he'll mark against them. If the horse is correct and there seems to be no reason for the splint, he'll no doubt assume it was caused by a blow to the leg, or some other type of injury.

The chest of a halter horse should be well V'd, with the legs extending straight down from the chest and shoulder area. A strong chest is an asset to a halter horse, but extreme width is looked down on. A horse that is horribly wide and too heavily muscled in the front end will travel like a jack hammer.

The way a horse travels counts a great deal. A judge is looking for a pretty mover, one which can get from "point A" to "point B" without excess wear and tear on his legs. If he wings or paddles as he moves, or travels close and hits one leg with the other, he is a candidate for unsoundness. He must travel straight and true, with the back feet following in the same line as the tracks made by the front feet.

THE YOUNG HALTER PROSPECT

Choosing a "baby" to halter isn't easy, because some things will change as he grows and some won't. But the fact remains that if this baby is BALANCED, he will remain that way.

When you go out into a pasture to look at the foals with their mothers, stand way back and look at how all the pieces fit— then divide each foal visually into thirds and look again.

Watch the way the foal travels. If the youngster is normal, he's curious about your presence. If you stay back from him and crouch low to the ground or down on one knee, he's almost

Owner Burl Flanigan made a good choice in this futurity colt. The youngster placed in the prestigious Cow Palace Weanling Futurity, shown by Paul Silva.

certain to begin coming toward you. You can see how straight he travels when he's walking *naturally*. A young horse that's not well halter broke and is being dragged along somewhat when led out for you to see will certainly not be showing you his natural way of moving.

Too many horse owners choose the most heavily muscled baby in the pasture to halter. They want the one who looks most adult. You should be wary of the foal that seems *too* well developed and proportioned, who has matured very early in life. A baby should look like a baby, and not like a four-year-old. Some horses that start out early with tank-like bodies and bulges everywhere don't develop the length of leg necessary to carry that big body. The bodies get bigger and longer and the legs don't. Before long, you have a fifteen hand Dachshund.

Look for the presence of inside gaskin muscle on a young horse. While you can build up the outside gaskin, to a certain degree, with exercise, you can't make inside muscle appear when it's not there to begin with.

Look for correctness in legs. If a 90-day-old baby is straight and true, he's going to stay that way, if you take care of his feet and exercise him well. If a colt does not exercise on his own, or is not taken out of his small area to work, his shoulder muscles won't develop and he'll take on a splay footed stance to compensate for the lack of support in his shoulders. Be sure your choice is exercised correctly so he'll stay straight.

Consider all the basics that were discussed on overall correctness of the general halter horse in judging the foal. Look at the baby and see if everything balances and ties in together. Expect him to grow, lengthen and refine, and lose that "baby boxcar" look. Always keep in mind that BALANCE is the key. Refinement, muscle definition, breediness, correctness of legs and a good way of traveling all tie in and give you the halter horse that can win.

Futurities are big, and they are tough. Cow Palace futurities, such as this one, have had over 100 entries in the bigger years.

Chapter 3

Formulating Feed and Worming Programs

It is well known around the horse industry that horses in general are fed an excessive amount of food supplements, and it appears that halter horses are at the head of that list. Too many owners of halter horses don't follow feeding directions or check food rations for duplications of vitamins. In fact, instead of feeding *balanced* rations, if owners hear that one cup of something will make a coat shiny, they'll feed the horse *three* cups of it for good measure!

If you use supplements, such as coat conditioners and all-around vitamin–mineral preparations, you *must* follow directions. To overdose a horse on supplements can cause vitamin toxicosis.

Once a horse has his growth and is in good condition, you'll find that many veterinarians will advise you to feed just a good balanced ration and forget about all of the "extras." One such veterinarian once had me replace coat supplements with small amounts of soybean meal and sea kelp in the grain ration. The results were gratifying.

The wonderful aspect of owning a horse today is that the large reputable feed companies have done all the work, all the research and all the mixing, and they can give you rations designed for specific needs. In most cases, explicit directions on amounts to feed come with these mixes. One example is Purina Big 'Un, a foal feed you can mix with Purina Omalene. The two, when fed with pasture or high quality hay, give a foal all that is needed to grow. There is no need to add supplements. Feeding has been simplified.

If you decide to mix your own feeds, the first thing you have to establish is the horse's needs with regard to the classification it falls into. Is it a mare in foal? A mare nursing a foal? Possibly you have a foal you want to creep feed, or one that is weaned. Yearlings are fed differently, then there are the two-year-olds. Possibly you have an adult horse. This can be one that is working hard, or one that is fairly idle. Establish which category your horse falls into, then look at the requirements. You must also look at your horse as an individual, as some are easier keepers than others. If you are not going to use commercial feeds and want to mix your own, I highly suggest that you work with

Feed your horse as an individual.

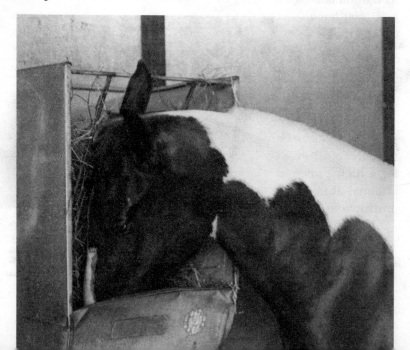

a veterinarian on establishing a ration that will help your horse meet all his requirements and will take advantage of the type of feeds that are most nutritious and available in your own area. Some types of land, for example, have soil which is low in the substances necessary for growing good pasture. In this event, supplementation and differences in rations would likely be advisable.

BROODMARES

During early gestation, the needs of the broodmare aren't as great as those of the last trimester—or final 90 days before foaling. Fetal development at this late stage is extremely rapid. Some broodmares become terribly fat during pregnancy because owners overfeed, feeling that they're "eating for two." If a mare begins to drop weight because of her body giving so much to the foal, her feed ration should, naturally, be increased, but care should be taken that she not get too fat and out of condition before foaling.

If you have a broodmare that weighs 1200 pounds, you can figure roughly that she should have a *minimum* of twelve pounds per day of good hay, preferably alfalfa which is high in protein. Many mares aren't easy keepers and require twice the amount in order to maintain the correct weight. For a mare of this size, about six pounds of a good, professionally mixed and balanced feed, such as Omalene, will give adequate nutrition. During the last 90 days of gestation, the sweet feed is increased to 6½ pounds or more per day and the addition of a high protein feed such as Purina Horse Charge, or Calf Manna, at one or two pounds per day (according to package instructions) is added.

After foaling, the mare's needs increase as she must now produce milk. Chances are she will also be rebred, so she will be nursing one foal and "building" the next. At this point, her hay ration goes up to a *minimum* of 15 pounds per day (more if she's dropping weight) and sweet feed is up to 15 pounds daily. If feeding Horse Charge, the amount goes up to 2½ pounds, or two pounds of Calf Manna. Remember that the mare reaches her peak of lactation at six weeks and her system is most taxed at that time. After the peak, milk production decreases. This is one reason why studies have been done to encourage early weaning.

CREEP FEEDING FOALS

Again, I stress that commercial foal feeds are probably the safest feeds to use. Many problems can occur with foals due to an imbalance in the phosphorus/calcium ration. The best way to avoid such problems is to rely on commercial foal feeds.

Foals, such as this new colt sired by Bright Chip, will get a head start through creep feeding.

For this reason, I will not dwell on the exact requirements of the young foal, as trying to mix your own "magic brew" all too often results in overfeeding, over-supplementing and damage to the foal.

With halter foals, we are after early growth, absence of problems, successful weaning, and marketability. The best way to start is to begin creep feeding the foal at two weeks of age, earlier if he shows an interest. The best way to start is to *teach* the foal to eat by placing some grain directly into his mouth. In the case of mixtures such as Big 'Un or Omalene, a small amount, especially of a sweet feed like Omalene, would likely tempt the foal to eat the feed himself after sampling some put into his mouth.

During the first six months, the foal is growing at a higher rate than at any other time of his life. He will gain up to four pounds per day. This is why creep feeding is so essential at this time, especially if you have a foal that is nominated for a weanling futurity. Don't wait until *after* weaning to get that growth. Help the foal while he's still nursing. Be sure to build some sort of creep feeder so that "Mother" doesn't get all of the feed intended for the foal.

All too often, young foals miss one very important vitamin . . . none other than Vitamin D. This is something to give a foal besides creep feed. Let him grow up with the benefit of three hours a day, or more, of sunshine. Vitamin D is necessary for proper skeletal development. This development is closely related to soundness, and we all want our horses to be sound long after they've reached that futurity.

WEANING

There are many different opinions on when to wean foals, but the fact remains that the creep fed foal will fend better in weaning than one who has been relying solely on the mare's milk. Foals also suffer less of a weight loss if stress is kept to a minimum. If foals are weaned in pairs, or groups, eating becomes competitive and they rarely lose their appetites.

Old standards on weaning saw foals taken away from the mares at age four to six months. My first experiment with earlier weaning was with a Paint colt, Rodeo Cowboy, who was weaned at age three months. For lack of another foal to put him with, he was left alone, but fretted very little and was eating his grain ration almost immediately after his mother was taken away. At the age of six months, he was placed under all three judges in a Paint weanling colt futurity, with 35 entered. As a weaned foal, he was fed commercial foal feeds and alfalfa hay, and no additional supplements except for oil for his coat. He grew well with no setbacks from being weaned at three months. At age two, he stands 15.1½ hands and is still growing.

This year, we will wean our foals even earlier, trying a theory introduced by the Department of Animal Science, University of Maryland. This is based on the theory that lactation of the mare reaches peak at six weeks and that, after that time, a foal depending greatly on mare's milk might actually lack some nutrition, when you consider the growth rate that is prevalent at this time. This study was based on the fact that early weaning and proper feed and supplementation may actually increase the development of the foal.

During this study, several foals were monitored, among them two which were weaned at two months of age and two at the age of six months. According to a report on the study, "All foals received a diet of approximately 19 per cent protein. The diets of two of the treatment groups, one two-month weaning group and one six-month weaning group, received a 19 per cent ration with 20 per cent of the diet consisting of Borden's Foal Lac, a commercial milk replacer. The ration was fed at liberty, with constant access to water and hay."

Weights and heights of the foals were recorded weekly. The earlier weaned foals were supplemented also with antibiotics, which were given orally in the feed rations. "Both antibiotics showed trends of increasing feed efficiencies . . ." according to the study.

The summary of the study stated that early weaning was shown to be economical and beneficial to both the mare and the foal. The early weaned foals showed better weight gains than those not weaned until six months of age, yet by the yearling year, the two groups seemed to equalize as the ones weaned at six months *caught up*. Supplementation with milk replacers seemed to be what made the difference and produced early gains. If you have a weanling which you are raising for a futurity, early weaning might be your answer.

Yearlings and Two-Year-Olds

During the study on early weaning, the protein level of the foals was held at nineteen per cent. According to William J. Tyznik, Ph.D., Ohio State University, the protein needs of a horse drop with age. At the California Livestock Symposium, Dr. Tyznik stated, "After the foal reaches six months of age, the protein level can be dropped to 16 or 18 per cent depending on the quality of hay and/or pasture the foal is consuming. From one year until two years of age, a 16 per cent ration should be maintained. Anything the horse will be in size has pretty much been established by the time a horse is two years old. At this time, the protein content can be lowered to 14 per cent or even 12 per cent, providing immature forage is being fed."

If one of these young horses is on a special regimen to produce a well fit horse, the protein percentage may have to be increased. You'll find, however, that halter horses don't work nearly as hard as most people think. When you look at the twenty or thirty minutes per day put on a yearling, for instance, and compare it to the several hours of hill climbing a ranch horse puts in while gathering cattle, you'll see why so many "outsiders" say our halter horses are overfed and underworked.

No, we can't and don't ride our yearlings or two-year-olds and work them like ranch horses. Therefore, they should be fed according to the work they do.

Again, I suggest using commercial feeds which have directions on feeding according to the horse's weight. Loading excess weight on yearlings and two-year-olds will only cause soundness problems.

THREE YEARS AND UP

According to Dr. Tyznik, "Horses reach maturity at about three years of age and at this point in time, ten to twelve per cent protein will serve adequately." He states that there are exceptions, such as heavily working horses and nursing mares, who require higher levels of protein.

WORKING ON THE COAT

If you're mixing your own grains, I would strongly suggest you consult a veterinarian who can tell you which grains in your area are of the highest quality and in what levels they should be fed to your horse as an *individual*. When you do consult him, you might also ask about the use of the following coat supplements in the feed:

Standard Commercial Coat Supplements   Preparations such as Dia-glo, available through veterinarians, are a tremendous help in producing a good hair coat quickly.

Soybean Meal   High in protein and fed at the rate of just one measuring cup per day by most halter fitters, this is an excellent "boost" for a hair coat.

Sea Kelp   A half cup of sea kelp added to the grain ration daily will help produce a good coat. Care must be taken not to overfeed this additive.

Oils   A great many halter horse fitters add oil to the grain ration to help produce a sheen in the coat. The best types to use are those made up of unsaturated fats, such as corn oil or safflower oil. The minimum amount fed should be two ounces (*two* tablespoons fed *twice* daily), more if you're working on a poor coat. Within 30 to 40 days, the coat should show excellent improvement.

Remember that grooming adds greatly to the quality of the hair coat, as does a proper parasite control program. You can feed all the coat supplements you want, but if you don't worm your horse and don't groom him regularly, he won't have a maximum quality hair coat.

OTHER NECESSITIES

Water and salt are essential to the horse. Clean, fresh water should be available at all times, and containers should be checked regularly to be sure that no foreign matter is in the water.

Salt is often added, in balance, to commercial feeds. If it isn't, and you are adding loose salt, it should not exceed 1 per cent of the weight of your grain mix. The best way to provide

Hay . . .   *pellets . . .*   *or cubes?*

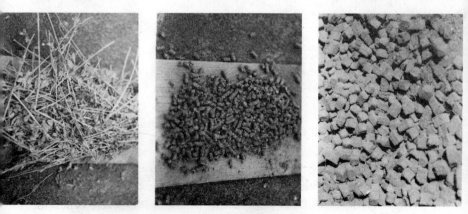

salt is through the use of a block to which the horse has free access.

HAY, PELLETS OR CUBES?

Opinions vary on which is best. Many feel that the absence of hay decreases belly size. Others feel that feeding cubes or pellets does not make that much difference in the belly, but they feed these for the sake of convenience and easy availability when good hay cannot be found. The only way to tell which will work for a horse as an individual is to experiment. Just remember these facts about each.

If you feed alfalfa, it should be leafy, green, dust free and have an aromatic smell. Look for the shorter stemmed alfalfa, with a great deal of leaf. Not only is it nutritious, but horses can eat it more leisurely than cubes or pellets and will often be quieter and more content during the day than if they "wolf down" pellets quickly and have nothing left to munch on.

Many of the commercial pellets, which are alfalfa based, contain a great deal of grain. You may determine this by reading the labels. If you think a pellet is mostly alfalfa but it isn't, and you don't decrease your grain ration, you'll be over-graining your horse.

Alfalfa cubes are in use a great deal on the West Coast. Care must be taken that these are dust free, green and free from mold. There is also the danger of a horse choking on a cube, particularly if the cubes are being fed in a trailer manger, and this must be considered. If a horse is nervous about being hauled and his throat becomes dry, much as yours would in a stress situation, he *can* choke on cubes.

THE EASY KEEPER

What if you're feeding a commercial sweet feed and your horse seems to be gaining too quickly? You may wish to keep the same poundage in your grain ration, substituting rolled or crimped oats for half of the sweet feed. This gives the horse enough energy to work without accumulating excess fat, depending, naturally, on the amount of daily work he is receiving. Chapter Seven contains a feed formula for reducing the obese horse.

FEED MANAGEMENT

How you feed is just as important as *what* you feed. One of the main killers of horses is colic, and care must be taken to prevent it. Dr. Gary Potter of Texas A & M spoke at the California Livestock Symposium and outlined the following tips for colic prevention through proper management. He felt that the following of these practices would help prevent 99 per cent of all colics:

1. Keep the horse as worm-free as possible, paying special attention to freeing him of bloodworms.
2. Be careful to feed regularly.
3. Don't over-gorge your horse with carbohydrates.
4. Don't fill your horse with indigestible or poorly digestible fibrous hay that his body can't absorb.

PARASITE CONTROL

Horse owners seem to go one way or the other with worming programs. Either they worm far too often, which can in some cases result in liver damage over a long term, or they don't worm enough. For this reason, the very best program you can establish is one of "check first, worm second." The fecal examination costs very little and tells a lot. When you first get a horse in for halter fitting, take a manure sample to your vet and have him look at it through a microscope. He can easily tell which types of parasites the horse has and what stage they are in. Then he can prescribe a wormer.

*Through regular fecal exams and prescribed wormings with a "gun,"
the author has kept Rodeo Cowboy free of harmful parasites.*

Some wormers are extremely safe, with safety margins up to a thirty-times overdose factor. Others aren't so safe. Young horses seem to need worming at more frequent intervals, so if your vet prescribes a safe, mild wormer, you may be able to use it as often as every thirty days on your foals and yearlings without causing problems. You must still continue consulting your vet, and continue the fecal examinations, for some worming preparations cause an immunity, when used over and over again, and the worms could wiggle by without being affected.

Set these rules of parasite control:

1. When your foal is six weeks of age, take a fecal sample to your veterinarian and ask what to use and when to begin.
2. Follow the frequency of worming established by your vet. He'll probably be glad to outline a program for you.
3. Be very careful about worming broodmares during the first and last three months of gestation. Some wormers are damaging at these times.

4. With mature horses, have a fecal examination run every four to six months, worming accordingly. If *sanitary* conditions are poor, do it more often.

SANITARY CONDITIONS

The parasite cycle is vicious. A wormy horse drops the eggs along with the manure and along comes a "clean" horse and grazes on a lovely batch of grass—infested with worm eggs. You now have *two* wormy horses. How do you avoid it?

If you have permanent pasture, don't turn any horse out to graze until it has a "clean" fecal check showing that there's no parasite activity in its body.

Clean your corrals and stalls regularly. Put manure in a compost pile and let it decompose for at least two weeks before it is spread in open areas, pastures, etc. This will kill any eggs which are present.

Establish a holding pen. Don't bring a new horse that may be wormy into any stall or corral where other worm-free horses will be put later. You'll be reinfesting your "clean" horses. Keep the new horse in the holding pen until he has been wormed and fecals clean, then you can put him in with your other horses.

Pray for frost! Frost does a good job of killing worm eggs which are on the ground. In years when frost is minimal or absent, worm infestation reaches a peak.

Chapter 4

Training the Halter Horse

Halter training begins when a foal is with the mother, particularly if you plan on taking that baby to a halter futurity as a weanling. Early handling then is imperative. And, if it's done right, respect is instilled immediately and the horse is started out in the right direction.

You can halter a baby at just a few days old, while he's still small enough to control easily. In a stall or a corral corner, pen the foal and grab the base of his tail with one hand, putting your other arm around the front of his chest. Lift the tail in the air and hold the colt as though you were preparing to pick him up. As you restrain him, a helper can put a halter on him.

Using a rope around the rump, and one from the halter, encourage the foal to take a few steps at a time, then call the lesson quits. Don't leave the halter on as, left unattended, an inquisitive foal can become hooked on a fence or some protruding material and seriously injure himself.

When a foal is a few weeks old and has had some lessons in leading, you can begin handling his feet. The best way to make a foal understand where to put his feet is to put them there for him. You might choose to work five minutes a day with the baby and, possibly at first, only place his front feet. You can do this as he stands next to his mother, and he'll be relaxed about the entire situation.

HALTER BREAKING OLDER FOALS

Many people do catch their foals to worm them and give inoculations at an early age, but they don't begin halter breaking until later. Sometimes there are so many foals to be handled on one ranch that one or another foal at the end of the list will have reached a powerfully resistant size at just a few months of age. What do you do then, especially if you're not "blessed" with bionic strength?

One breeding farm in California quite often uses a pony horse to help in halter breaking the larger foals. They begin by tying the mare in the stall, and tying the foal next to her to learn about pressure on the halter. Then, when the foal is ready to be actually led, he has some idea of what's to come.

Doris Sharp, who along with her husband Eugene owns Halcyon Farms, has a big, stout pony horse that will tolerate just about anything. Many of the foals at Halcyon have grown to nearly yearling size though still on their mothers because of the early growth that is a mark of the Halcyon sire, Bright Chip. So Doris has learned that it's hard to wrestle with a large foal after it's a few months old. For this reason, she attaches a twelve foot rope to the foal's halter and uses the pony horse as "leverage."

Dallying to the saddle horn, being careful not to catch her fingers in the dally, Doris begins walking the pony horse out and the foal is encouraged to come forward. It's natural for a foal to set back then leap forward, but after learning that it is easier to give to the pull than resist it, the baby generally comes right along. After a few sessions with the pony horse, it's easy to lead the foal from the ground.

THE WEANED FOAL

At Fabulous Farms in Watsonville, California, Lynn and Harry Stickler hold off most of the serious halter breaking un-

Doris Sharp halter breaks the larger foals at Halcyon Farms by using a stout pony horse.

til the foals are weaned. For this reason, it's not unusual to see a dozen weanlings tied to the fence in a long line, all learning about halters at the same time.

One at a time, the foals are haltered and a belly rope with a solid knot is secured around the weanling's middle. It comes up between the front legs and is run through the halter. Then this rope is tied to a stout fence, as is a regular lead rope snapped to the halter. Leaving the colts tied in this way for long periods of time establishes a healthy respect for the halter. After setting back a few times and feeling pressure on both his head and the barrel area, a colt soon learns to give in to the pressure. It is safest to tie the colt fairly high up, higher than his withers, to prevent injury to his neck if he should set back hard on the ropes.

Lynn Stickler settles a weanling as it receives a lesson in halter pressure by being tied to the fence. The belly rope discourages pulling back.

LEADING OUT

When a young halter prospect is ready for serious schooling and is leading well with a halter and rope, the Sticklers use a

Harry Stickler holds the "come-along" he uses in schooling his halter horses.

"come-along" made of a leather nose band from an old halter and a chain with a large snap. The accompanying photos show how this is put on the horse's head. The horse in the pictures is a yearling daughter of the Sticklers' stallion, Ben Bar.

This is how the Sticklers rig the come-along on the head. The filly is a daughter of their AQHA stallion, Ben Bar.

Caution must be taken in the use of any schooling device, particularly a chain. Whenever you use one to take hold of the horse, you must *instantly release it*. If done too hard and not quickly released, the pressure put on a horse by the device will often cause it to rear over backwards. However, it doesn't hurt to take a good hold, and release, so that the horse comes off his front feet just a little. In this way you know you have corrected him hard enough to get his attention.

When Harry corrects a horse with the chain, he uses instant release.

Harry Stickler uses this come-along to get his halter horses to lead out promptly. Again, this is done by taking hold of, then instantly releasing, the horse's head. This is a great help in getting the young horses to trot right out when they are asked. If they don't come to you, you get after them.

The come-along is a fine tool to use in teaching a horse to lead out promptly.

TEACHING THE TIGHT TURN

While the current rage is for a judge to have you walk toward him, set up the horse, then trot away, many judges are still using the old standards of halter classes, which consist of walking up, turning, and trotting back. The reason for the walking and trotting is for the judge to see how straight and true your horse travels. Is he winging or paddling, or does he travel straight as an arrow? If you have a *good* halter horse, he does travel correctly and you certainly want the judge to notice you. For this reason, you must walk and trot a straight line . . . precisely straight. In the case of the walk-down, turn and trot-back, you plant the horse's back end, move his rear around, and when he is turned and ready to trot back, he is in the *exact* same tracks that he walked down in. He had walked *straight* to the judge and now he's going to trot *straight* away in those same tracks. The judge doesn't have to move to see him. The horse will travel better than he would if you swerved a big circle turn and came in at an angle, pulling on the horse to straighten him up.

For a tight turn, the horse needs to move almost like a stock horse that's doing a turn. The hind end remains in place, and the front end pivots around it. The Sticklers' come-along works very well in teaching the horse to move *lightly* around, with very little pressure put on the head.

Harry Stickler first stops the horse, then moves his hand under the chin to the opposite side of the horse. Standing on the left, his hand going under the horse to the right encourages it to move away from him. The final product is a horse that is so light that when you begin to move into him and shift your hand, he rocks around.

If you get a horse that takes the room of a semi truck to turn around, you can use a fence to encourage him to turn. With the fence to the right of him and you on the left, position him so that he is parallel to the fence, about four feet away from

To teach the horse to turn, Harry first positions his hand under the chin, then pushes it to the right side of the horse to move the front end around.

In teaching the tight turn, lead the horse down the fence line.

Stop and back one or two steps to rock him back on his hindquarters.

Turn him toward the fence and walk him back down the line. Notice how Joanie Cohn has Hug N Tuff turning off his right hind leg (the pivot foot).

it. Walk him down the fence, stop, back him a couple steps to rock him back on his hindquarters, and turn him toward the fence, doing a complete half turn so that you've "swapped ends." This teaches him to rely on his rear end to work off of in the turn and the fence stops him from trying to move forward and make a big circle.

THE STOP

Regardless of the way a halter class is judged, whether it's walking and trotting a straight line or incorporating a turn, at some point in the class you're going to have to stop that horse in front of the judge. The ideal way is to teach the horse to stop when *you* stop. In the show ring, if you have to take hold of him and jerk his head to stop, he'll throw it up in the air and more than likely spraddle his back feet, stopping spread out and with little or no chance of getting into a good square stance quickly.

The straight legged, well put together halter horse will stop naturally straight and true and need little adjustment in his stance IF he's stopped lightly and not pulled off balance.

Stopping schooling begins from the walk, using the come-along, a lead shank over the nose, or some other effective device that will make him a believer in stopping. It's best to begin working along a fence to encourage him to stop straight. Walk him out, stop yourself, and say "whoa." In the beginning, you'll have to take hold of him to show him that he should stop when you do. Don't expect him to learn that in one day; it takes awhile. You might try a few stops during the day, and when you get the best stop with the least amount of effort on your part, rub the horse on the neck, loosen the come-along and put him away for the day as a reward.

Each time you bring the horse out to work him, be sure to do it until the point gets across, then end on a happy note. If he's being belligerent in the beginning and you have to use

In teaching the stop, begin by leading the horse down the fence line.

Say "whoa" and take hold of him.

several jerk and release type pulls, do it. Get after him until he begins stopping instantly. When he *does* stop lightly on the word "whoa," that's when to pet him and put him away.

The word "whoa" is only used in the beginning as a transition from using the shank to having him stop on his own. When you can abandon jerking on the shanks and the horse will stop on "whoa," begin working on having him stop because *you* stop. Walk him down, and stop yourself. If he keeps going forward, tell him "whoa" and if you have to, go back to using the shank. He should know the word "whoa," because some day when you're in a show ring and he's drifting off and not paying complete attention, you might be able to get him to stop with a solid voice command, rather than doing much with his head. This, of course, is only for "mild" cases of not paying attention, because if he is seriously bad in the show ring, you'll have to use the shank.

Try, however, to walk him down, and later trot him, and encourage him to stop when you do. The same will happen with the turn around: when he sees you begin to move, he'll move also. When a halter horse is working light, on a loose shank and responds instantly, it presents a better picture to a judge.

First Stand Still ...

"Whoa" comes into play here, also, because the horse needs to know that the word means "stop all motion and hold it right there." If your horse learns to square up, it's not going to be worth anything if he doesn't learn to stand still. And when the horse is trying to learn all about leading out, stopping and turning, teaching him also to stand still doesn't clutter his mind, but gives you something else to work on, rather than drilling him all morning on just leading and turning.

Yes, he has to stop before he can stand, so lead your horse out a ways, stop him, and don't worry about *how* he is standing, as long as you can keep him still. Keep telling him "whoa," over

Teach him to stand still before you teach him to square up. "Whoa" is the most important word in the vocabulary of the halter horse. If he'll obey this word, you can always control him in a spooky class situation.

and over again, and if he starts moving around, give a pull and release the shank or come-along to reinforce that word. Each time he moves when you don't want him to, get after him just enough to make him get "on the muscle" (tensed up and alert to his movements) and *want* to stay put, but don't run him back. You're trying to keep him in *one spot*. After he's been on the muscle and you've gotten after him, hopefully he'll learn to relax and still stay put. Remember that this isn't an overnight learning experience: and it takes more time with some horses than with others.

Don't practice by standing your horse still in only one spot and for a long period of time. Walk him out again, stop him and let him stand somewhere else. With the young horse, you may want to have him stand for only three or four minutes before you move him again. The point you're trying to get across is that wherever you tell him to "whoa," he should stop and stand still until you take him away.

Work on standing still also helps greatly in getting a horse used to lining up with others. If you can get two people to help you, have them line their horses up on each side of him, a safe distance away. Make your horse stand still. Then line the three up "head and tail" with your horse in the middle. Again, be careful to allow enough space so that your horse, or one of the others, can't kick and injure someone.

Hug N Tuff stands square in a practice session.

Bring the horses back side to side again, and have one of the horses led out, turned around and trotted back. If you try to simulate everything that might happen in a show ring, you'll both be ready for it when you get there.

Then Stand Square

Standing with all fours in a good square position is unnatural for a horse. While a straight legged, well balanced horse will stop pretty square when he's led and stopped, if he were out on his own he wouldn't stay this way for very long. He'd naturally shift a foot to get comfortable, or cock a leg. The main thing you must understand about teaching a horse to stand up for halter is that you *are* dealing with a position that is uncomfortable for a horse at first. As you repeatedly place his legs squarely under him and the muscles become oriented, it will gradually become a comfortable position for him, but it does take time. Once the horse learns that the position is now a comfortable one, he won't raise much fuss about it and will stand up quickly.

There are several ways to begin teaching a halter horse to stand square. The two-person method consists of one person holding the horse, while the other places the feet. This can be done with a halter and lead rope, or with a come-along, depending on how much resistance the horse wants to put up.

You may also want to use your voice in the beginning and tell the horse to "stand up" as you place the feet. You can abandon the voice command later, after the horse has graduated and learned to work off the halter.

Another method of teaching a horse to stand square is done while the horse is standing in the cross ties. This can be handled by one person, as the head is stationary and the horse can't go anywhere. California trainer Al Anderson has all his horses stand square in the cross ties during both daily groomings. He begins by hand placing their feet, as long as it takes for the

Using teamwork to teach a horse to square up is an effective means of schooling the halter horse.

horse to get the idea. He does this not only as a way to school the horse, but also as a safety measure for himself. If a horse is standing square on all fours, he's less likely to kick you than he is standing with a foot cocked.

STANDING SQUARE OFF THE HALTER

When you begin working from the halter, rather than hand placing legs, you can use two ropes. Put one regular lead rope on the halter, and also use a chain lead shank, with the chain under the chin of the horse. If the horse becomes a problem during schooling, such as getting nippy or not paying attention, you can correct him by pulling down on the chain and releasing instantly.

If you used your voice during hand placing, telling him to "stand up," your horse will have an idea of what's going on

By using both a bull rope and chain shank during schooling, you have the use of the chain to reinforce, but don't have to use it constantly.

when you begin working off the halter. Go ahead and talk to him in the beginning, until he learns to work off the halter alone.

Start by setting the hind legs first. Lead him up, then stop him. One hind foot will no doubt need adjustment, will have to be brought either forward or back. Let's say the right hind foot is a little too far forward of the left. You want to move that foot, and only that foot, at this time. Take the lead rope, close to the halter and pull it slightly to the left, *away* from the foot you want to move. This takes the weight off the side you're trying to position. When the horse moves the foot back where it should be, tell him "whoa" and give a slight pull down on the shank to plant the foot and lock it into position. Now, keep telling him "whoa," and rub his neck to let him know he did this correctly.

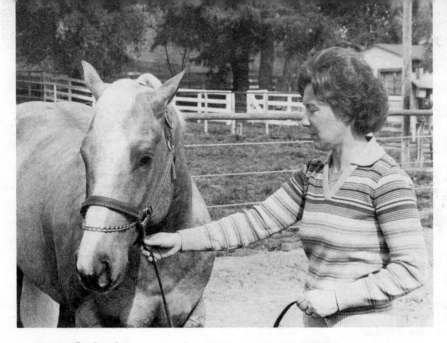

To set the hind legs, use a low pull, moving the head away from the leg that must be moved. This takes the weight off the leg and the horse will move it readily.

When you begin on the front feet, the same basics are true except that you will be lifting the head more to encourage a front foot to come up and move. By not lifting the head when you worked on the hind feet, you encouraged the horse to stay down solid on his front end and move only his back feet. But now you want to move the front feet, so you lift and shank up and pull the horse's head to the *opposite* side from the foot you want to move. As you lift his head, you bring it slightly forward or back, depending on whether the foot to be moved is to be brought forward to line it with the other, or moved back.

This is the final goal . . . to have a horse that will work lightly off the halter. In days past, you might have seen halter exhibitors kicking a horse's leg to get him to move it. You might have seen hand placing of the feet in classes, or someone smacking a leg with the leather end of the shank. That may be acceptable

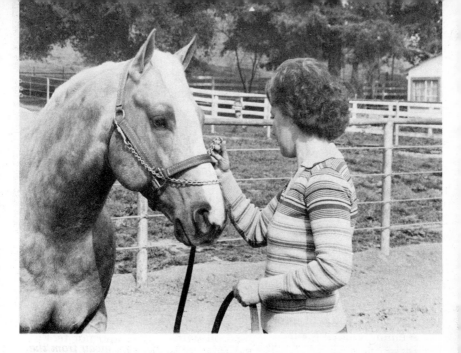

To move a front foot, lift the head up, then to the side opposite the foot to be moved.

in some cases, but rule books for such as the American Quarter Horse and the Pinto Associations prohibit the touching of a horse below the shoulder during a halter class. It stands to reason that other breed associations will follow. Many exhibitors in the past could get away with wrenching around and hand placing crooked front feet and twisting hocks, producing a horse that looked straight but really wasn't. This isn't acceptable in most cases today. The current method of holding many classes excludes this type of horse and handler right now.

Maybe you used to have a long time in the line-up with the others to stand your horse up square before the judge came to look at you. Many judges have become wise and are asking that the horses, one at a time, be led in at a walk, straight to the judge. The horse is then squared up, right before the judge's eyes, and it must be done quickly, efficiently, and without "cheating." The judge looks at the horse, then asks that it be trotted off. If you don't have a horse that will stand square and true by working off the lead shank alone, and one that will do it quickly, you'll be hurting yourself in the show ring.

ABANDON CHAINS AND COME-ALONGS

All the "encouraging" head gear used during schooling was there to produce a light horse that would move out of respect for you, the handler. In the beginning, it's easier to teach a horse with a shank or come-along than it is to be pulling and jerking at a halter noseband with a cotton rope. You simply have more control and more influence training with a shank or come-along. If you continue to use it, however, on an every-day basis, you will *lose* lightness and produce a horse who can seemingly have his head jerked off with a chain and not feel a thing. You're going to need lightness on the head when you take the horse to the show ring, especially if you are showing a stallion that needs some extra "help" from head gear.

Using a regular halter and a "bull rope" will suffice for every-day work. There's no reason to put a shank on a horse every time you take him out of the stall. If he gets out of hand, whack him on the sides with the bull rope, which should have a good sized knot tied in the end. Get him on one side and, if neces-sary, on the other, just to let him know he's in trouble, and that you have him contained. This method will scare him into sub-mission without having to jerk on his head with a shank and take away all the "feel."

Chapter 5

Care of the Feet and Legs

Since halter horses are so critically judged on their legs and feet, it is crucial that they be well taken care of. The old cliché that an ounce of prevention is worth a pound of cure most certainly applies in the case of the feet and legs of a halter horse.

Splint boots protect the legs as the horse works.

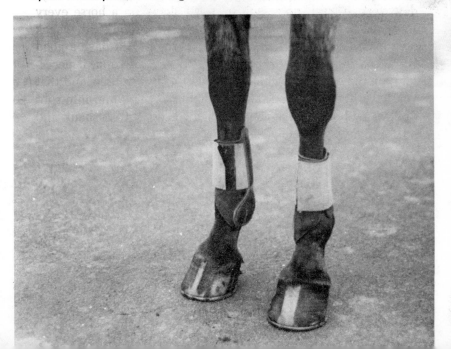

LEG CARE

A great deal of stress is put on the legs of a halter horse, and there is not only the danger of injury due to percussion against the ground, but the chance also exists that he will hit one leg with the other, causing a splint or other injury. To protect the front legs of your halter horse, never work him without splint boots. And, if he tends to stumble over himself, use bell boots. If you are concerned about back leg problems, wrap him with cotton and track wraps or Vetrap before workouts.

Following workouts, watch closely for any signs of swelling and soreness in the legs, particularly in the tendon area. When a horse is overworked, especially in the first stages of fitness, he is likely to suffer some soreness in the legs and may need to be wrapped. In this case, it never hurts to have a veterinarian prescribe some sort of liniment to help relieve the soreness. Because you will probably have to wrap the horse's legs, you need to be certain that the type of liniment you use *can* be used under wraps without blistering the horse.

Even if there is no visible sign of soreness in a horse's legs, you may wish to give him a rubdown from the knees and hocks to the coronary band, using regular rubbing alcohol if you feel he has had a strenuous workout. Slap those legs! Alternate your hands and rub vigorously in a downward motion. Keep rubbing until well after you see the veins begin to appear and protrude, for this will tell you that the circulation is at its peak.

If you want to "brace" your horse after a good workout, you can wrap him with a thick layer of cotton under the track or stretch wraps and leave the bandages on overnight. Take them off in the morning and give him another alcohol rub. Though a fit horse doesn't have too much trouble from hard work, a horse that is just beginning to work at a fitness program will likely be prone to a little soreness while his tendons and ligaments are becoming adjusted to the work. Be patient with him and give him every chance to keep those legs in good condition.

STOCKING UP

Quite often, when a horse has been brought in from pasture or a large corral and confined to a stall, he will have trouble with swelling in the legs, or "stocking up." You have to understand that when the horse was outside, moving constantly, there was good circulation in his legs. Now, confined to a small area, where movement is largely hindered, the resultant decrease in circulation will often cause swelling.

Some horses also stock up when shipped, such as trailering to a show, especially when going long distances. If your horse stocks up at home, or at a show before a class, simply try walking him out of it. The more he walks or trots, such as on a longe line, the more the swelling will go down. Alcohol rubs also help and, if you know you have a horse that tends to stock up while being trailered, rub his legs with alcohol and bandage over them for the trip. This will inhibit swelling. When you arrive at the show, remove the wraps, rub the legs, and walk the horse around.

WRAPPING YOUR HORSE'S LEGS

Unless you know how to properly wrap a horse, you can hinder rather than help him. The major cause of leg damage from improper wrapping is the misconception that a bandage must be extremely tight to offer support.

Wrapping too tightly can cause loss of circulation. When this is compounded by incorrect wrapping and not overlapping well, bandage bows can occur. Pressure from a tight, poorly wrapped bandage or a tie that is much too snug cuts the circulation off in a particular spot, or spots, on the leg. Then, when you remove the wraps, you will find a bump or ridge on the leg. This can sometimes be removed by heavy massage, but if it's too severe, it will require a poultice to bring it down. Imagine your disappointment when, arriving at a show for a halter class, you unwrap your halter horse's legs and find bandage bows! Learn to wrap correctly by practicing some "dry runs" before you go to a show, and you'll avoid problems for yourself and your horse.

The basic materials for wrapping legs consist of the padding and the actual wrap. You shouldn't use wraps only: the padding is very necessary. Padding can consist of sheet cotton, quilted or felt pads, and should always be of a material that will lay flat against the legs and not bunch up.

This leg was wrapped with sheet cotton and Vetrap. Photo courtesy of 3M.

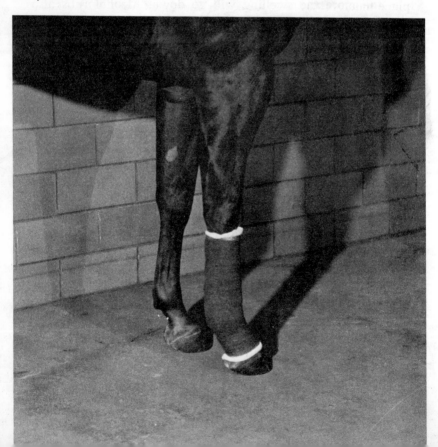

The actual wrap can be either regular track bandages, which have string-type ties or Velcro closures, or a stretch material such as Vetrap which clings to itself and needs nothing more to secure it at the end of the wrap. When using a stretch wrap, you must be careful not to wrap it too tightly. The correct way of judging the tension is to pull several inches away from the roll and, rather than stretching it to the fullest, letting it "relax" so that about half the tension is present . . . *then* wrap it on the leg. This has to be done with every wrap. Look at it much the same as wrapping an arm with an Ace bandage, with the realization that if stretched to its fullest and pulled tightly, circulation will be cut off. Used correctly, self-adhering wraps, such as Vetrap, are extremely advantageous, for they stay in place much better than conventional wraps.

Ready to Wrap?

Prepare your padding. Quilt pads should be folded once, lengthwise. Cotton, in sheets, is folded into thirds with the edges about an inch apart, smoothly tapering the pad and preventing any thick edges. When placing the pad or sheet cotton, it should be positioned vertically on the leg within an inch below the knee. The bottom should be no less than an inch above the coronary band. Should slippage occur, which is common, this placement will insure that adequate padding is still in place to supply the necessary support.

Be certain, when placing the padding, that there are no folds or pad ends on the back or front of the cannon bones. Whenever possible, place the folds of the padding on the side of the leg. Then, when beginning to cover with the wrap, tuck in about two inches of the track bandage or stretch wrap between folds of the padding.

The roll of the wrapping material should be placed facing the *outside* of the leg, so that you can easily unroll it as you wrap. Roll to the back, around the tendon, to the front and back again. You'll simply be circling the leg, being sure to leave at least one-half inch overlap with each circle. Remember that, with stretch wrap, you pull the spool out a few inches, relax it, then wrap.

Always begin at the middle of the leg, wrap down, then back up to the top. The most important pressure point is under the fetlock, particularly when shipping. When you reach this area, go under the back of the fetlock, then lift and wrap up, giving one firm wrap. Go around the leg again, then back under the fetlock for a second wrap. This will cause a V-shape of wrap in front of the bandage, because you were wrapping more down and up, than just around. By wrapping in this way, you will prevent any tight edges which might cut in to the front of the cannon bone.

After wrapping down, then up again, you should have some padding visible from the top and bottom of the wrap. If you're using track bandages, be sure to make your tie on the *side* of the leg, if it has string ties.

How long should you use the same wrap? As a rule of thumb, you should change wraps every twenty-four hours if a horse is wrapped due to injury. If you're shipping, you will naturally leave them on for the duration of the trip—but if it is a journey of several days, the legs should be *rewrapped* every twenty-four hours if at all possible.

FOOT OR HOOF CARE

Finding a competent shoer is first on any horseowner's list. When I've looked for one, I've always asked the best halter fitter I knew in the area for advice on who to use. A veterinarian is also a good source. They generally have farriers they contact in cases of foot problems, where they must work with a farrier to correct difficulties in a horse's feet.

Do take the time to investigate, because a bad farrier can ruin your halter horse. If the angle on the foot is wrong, your horse will travel badly, will have excess strain on his legs, and can possibly be very subject to stocking up. You naturally have to worry about harm to the horse, but you should also consider the fact that poor shoeing and trimming can lose you a class . . . even *all* your classes!

Especially with the young, growing horse, it is imperative that you maintain a well-balanced foot at all times. You need to begin trimming a foal as soon as the hooves become fairly firm, which could be as early as four or five weeks of age. The growth plates in the legs of the foals (the epiphyseal plates) are strongly affected by the hoof. If the hoof is level and correct, growth in the legs is the same. However, if one side of the hoof is lower or higher than the other, such as in the case of wearing down when a colt is worked a great deal in a circle, then the pressure is uneven and one side of the bone of the leg grows at a faster rate than the other.

Watch for this uneven wear in your young horses. If a hoof becomes unlevel and the colt isn't yet due for a complete trim, it might be wise to contact the farrier anyway and have him level the foot "in-between" complete trimmings.

Regular shoeing for older horses, and just trimming for the young, is an extremely important part of fitting halter horses. The old adage "No Foot, No Horse" is certainly true. Pay attention to what your horse's feet are trying to tell you. If you're working your young horse in a circle and he's wearing down the outsides of his feet, try ponying him more in a straight line. Have the unlevel feet corrected and work to keep them level. If your barefoot horse is chipping badly, ask your farrier to look at him. In the case of yearlings, especially the long yearlings, it is possible to put racing plates on the feet to keep them from bad wear. The heel nails are left off, allowing the foot to continue to grow and spread without restriction. Plating yearlings is often necessary in white legged horses with those incredibly soft pink hooves.

Daily Care of the Feet

Horses kept in stalls are prone to one of two evils: either the foot dries out badly from the turpentine content in the shavings, or the moisture from the stalls encourages thrush. For this reason, a hoof preparation, such as a mixture of Koppertox and regular household bleach, should be part of your halter horse kit. If the feet grow too slowly, or are soft and prone to breaking up, other preparations and "secret formulas" can be used. It's all part of the daily care.

Clean your horse's feet before and after you work him. It would be a shame to work him if you had skipped the cleaning and a foreign object had gotten lodged in his foot. It would also be a shame to put him back in the stall after working with something stuck in his foot.

There is much controversy about whether or not to use hoof dressings on the feet because of the normal intake and evaporation of moisture that occurs in the foot of the horse. Water seems to be one of the best conditioners for feet. It isn't always possible, however, to soak a horse's hooves in water. Most halter conditioners are using standard hoof preparations and having a great deal of success with them. Whether or not they should be used every day is another controversial subject, because some horse's feet are drier than others and warrant more care. To use hoof dressing daily, when it's not needed that often, seems a waste.

Many young horses that are exercised on a regular basis wear their feet down at almost a faster rate than they grow them. This is often true of white legged, pink-footed horses. These horses are often hoof sore because of the wear. The solution? Toughen the soles of the feet, and try to stimulate some extra growth.

To toughen the soles, brush regular turpentine on the sole only. Be careful not to let the turpentine run as the foot is held up, or it will run from the toe, up the front of the foot and into the coronary band which can make the skin sore.

Brushing the soles daily with turpentine helps toughen a tender foot.

Soaking the sole in a pie pan holding about an inch of turpentine also helps tender feet.

Not only can you brush the soles daily, but if the horse is sore and you *know* it's nothing more than excess wear causing the soreness, put about an inch of turpentine into a heavy tin pie plate. Put one foot in to soak for several minutes, while you hold the other foot up. Alternate and do all the feet. You'll find that most of the soreness, however, is generally in the front.

Strong iodine is another solution to use for painting the soles. This can be purchased from your veterinarian. Again, extreme caution should be used not to get this on the horse's skin, or on yours.

To stimulate growth, make a mixture of half Reducine and half Absorbine Hooflex. With a soft toothbrush, gently rub the mixture each day, or on alternate days, into the coronary band. This is an irritant, and by irritating the coronary band, the area from which growth of the hoof originates, growth is stimulated.

Daily, when you clean the horse's feet, check for the foul smell of thrush. This problem is not uncommon when horses are kept in box stalls, particularly if the stalls are often damp. Check along the sides of the frog. If thrush is bad, when you clean you'll often find the groove deeper than before. When you spot thrush, treat the bottom of the foot with Koppertox. You can also alternate, using that preparation one day and regular Clorox the next. If you're wondering about the extent of thrush, it can penetrate extremely deep in the foot. A horse we once purchased had it so bad that we had to soak cotton balls with Koppertox and shove them up deep inside the back of the frog/heel area of the foot with a screwdriver! Yes, thrush *can* be severe, and it can cause lameness.

There are many people who believe in miracle aids that will toughen the entire foot, especially for thin walled horses. Gelatin, added to the feed, was once thought of as having the miraculous power to improve a foot, yet research at some colleges and universities has shown that it has no such power and, if given in large doses, actually hinders the foot.

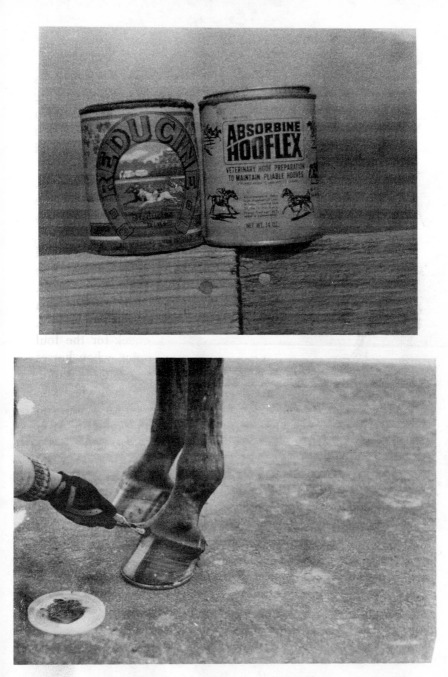

A half and half mixture of Reducine and Hooflex, applied to the coronary band on a regular basis, will stimulate foot growth.

Koppertox should be applied to combat a thrush condition.

Vitamins and feeds often claim to improve hoof texture almost overnight. False claims are prevalent in the horse world and advertised preparations should be checked out closely. While iodine or turpentine can toughen the sole, helping the problem, they don't change the makeup of the individual's hoof. Coronary band irritants help increase hoof growth, but the growth that comes out matches the type of foot that proceeded it. These solutions help you cope with the problem, but remember that no "miracle drug" or "miracle hoof preparation" is going to completely remanufacture a hoof. You sometimes have to learn to live with what you have, helping it along as best you can.

Chapter 6

Exercise—The Key to Fitness

The only way to fit and tone a horse's body is to give it *regular* exercise. And you have to increase the duration of the work as the horse becomes more fit, because the body reacts to stress. If you work a horse ten minutes a day at the same speed and level that you did in the beginning, there's no increase and no stress. You'll see some improvement, but certainly not as much as you will with a wise conditioning program.

Halter fitter Kenny Campbell of Texas believes that the key to telling when a horse has had enough exercise for one day is the presence of sweat. When you first start to work a horse, and he's been idle for a long time, he's going to tell you when he's tired. He's going to sweat and breathe at a faster rate than normal. Each day you work him, you'll find that the sweat takes a little longer to appear and that the hard breathing is delayed also. As the horse becomes fit, you'll also notice that his recovery rate is much faster. Where he used to take a long time to get back to breathing normally, when he's fit, he'll snap back faster. You'll be spending less time cooling him out.

When you use neck sweats, you'll find that the unfit horse will foam a great deal until he reaches some degree of fitness. From this point on, you'll see more of a clear sweat. Use all these indications of fitness to tell you just how much work to give a horse.

79

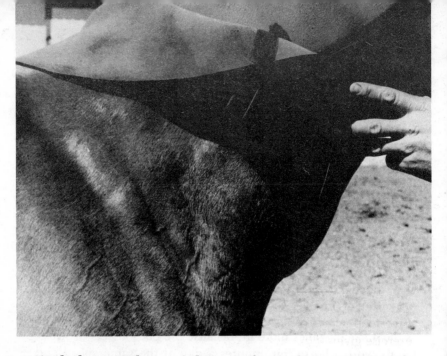

As the horse reaches some degree of fitness, the foaming sweat becomes a thing of the past and he develops a clear sweat.

Some halter trainers argue about which gait to use most in fitting a horse. Some say, "Trotting builds muscle, loping builds wind. We want muscle only so we'll trot him." But wind is important, too, for the horse has to be in a *total fitness* state to be able to withstand even a rigorous trotting schedule. If he can't breathe, he can't trot! It is known that if you want to build the muscles in the shoulder and forearm areas, extended trotting and forcing the horse to "reach" with each stride will develop these areas. If you're after muscling of the gaskin and hip area, backing the horse will do the most. That doesn't mean you *only* back him every day, or trot him, because *everything* needs to be worked—with special emphasis given to some areas more than others.

How about galloping? Many people are fighting saggy bottom lines on their halter horses. California's Tim Kane, who has produced many Appaloosa halter champions, asks the question,

"Have you ever seen a bellied-up race horse?" He believes in adding some galloping to the work schedule if the horse needs work on the bottom line.

Whichever gait you use, be sure to warm the horse up and get him ready for it. Spend some time walking before you trot, lope or gallop. Remember that our halter horses stand in stalls and don't move around much until we bring them out to work them. If a horse was worked hard one day and stalled until the next, he's going to be tight and a little sore in the beginning. Bring him out and walk him awhile before you go on, so he can loosen up and *feel* more like working.

When your horse finally does get fit, keeping him there is a matter of just being regular in his exercise. At the Fresno Livestock Symposium, Tommy Manion said that the amount of exercise given to his horses is decided on depending on the age and condition of the horse. "Our fit yearlings are worked every other day for twenty to thirty minutes. Naturally, an older horse can take more."

Some of us get so excited about weanling and yearling futurities, we overexert our young horses. Remember that they're babies, and treat them accordingly.

Whatever the age of your horse, you have a wide variety of ways to exercise him. Let's look at a few. Remember that you may have to use more than one to get the job done. Also, it never hurts to vary the exercise program constantly to keep a horse from becoming a basket case because of boring repetition!

First the Boots

Your first thought, whenever you exercise your horse, should be to put on splint boots to protect the legs. In round corrals especially, horses will often hit the side and need that leg protection. If you feel it necessary, you can also use bell boots.

If you lack splint boots, you may want to wrap the legs during work. Be careful to wrap them smoothly and give good support under the pastern.

THE HOT WALKER

The pros and cons of the hot walker need to be discussed for as many trainers hate them as those that swear by them. Looking first at the pros, consider the chance of exercising four horses at once. Also, if you lack a round pen or a place to pony or longe a horse, a hot walker comes in handy. If you are lucky, you have one with three speeds and a reverse gear so that the horses can be worked in both directions.

What are the cons? First, with a young horse, constantly working in a circle puts more stress on the outside of his foot

Steve Dal Porto puts a yearling Appaloosa colt on the hot walker. Notice the splint boots on the front legs.

as he moves and this can cause unequal stress up his leg. Too, if the ground around the walker is not completely level, the horse is not walking on a flat surface—causing even more unequal stress.

Horses are smart. They're stronger than the gears of the walker and they find out fast that they can stop the action by laying back a little on the tie rope. If you're not right there to move them out with a whip or a harsh comment, they can stand through an entire exercise session, listening to the walker motor hum a neutral tune.

PONYING

The advantages of ponying are many. Horses become very well mannered when they're worked from a pony horse. They

Hot walkers are fine . . . until a smart horse like this learns to stop them.

can be controlled well because you can box them in between the pony horse and an arena fence. You can climb hills, cross creeks and fly down a straightaway of a track. A good solid pony horse is no doubt the greatest asset to someone fitting halter horses.

What is a good pony horse? Ideally, it's a big one with enough power to control a dallied-up monster, but not so big and stout that it can't move well and climb hills. A pony horse is tolerant in that it must accept being bumped, sometimes kicked at, and bitten. A little shot of "cranky" should be added to the tolerance, because a pony horse that will pin his ears back and reach around to tell a colt to get back will keep you from constantly pulling on a colt to bring him back into position at your leg.

When you're ponying, it's a good idea to have two ropes. A lead shank with a chain will help you discipline a horse if he

Doris Sharp ponies a Bright Chip daughter. She much prefers pony-ing young horses, to working them in small circles.

gives you trouble, but you can't dally up and pull with a chain. So a second rope, about twelve feet long that is snapped into the halter, is also good to carry. Once a young horse has been ponied some, he'll become mannered enough that only one of the two ropes will be necessary.

If you pony your colt on a day when he's feeling high and wants to force his way beyond the front of the pony horse, start your session with the chain *over* his nose to easily shank him back to you. If he gets settled later, and even begins to drag a little, switch the chain to under his chin and pull him forward. With luck, you'll eventually be able to use only a regular lead rope, for the more you use a chain on a halter horse, the more "feel" he loses. Then, when you need to shank him in a class, he'll be numb. Use of the chain is a good schooling device, but it shouldn't be overused.

When you first begin ponying a horse, it may be worried about coming up close to the pony horse. Since your horse is positioned to the right of the pony horse, you can circle to the right and contain the horse to get him accustomed to being close to the pony horse. If he locks up and doesn't want to come forward at first, circling will help him also. And, so will the old "dally and pull 'em" technique. But dally only with a rope, *never* with a chain.

There are days that young horses feel like monsters when they come out of a stall. On days such as this, they'll rear, kick out, leap sideways and practice every maneuver they know until they settle down. If you don't want a horse like this to use up all that energy uncontrolled before you pony, then you have to work to contain him until he's settled. Pony him along a fence, so that the fence is on his right and the pony horse on the left, and work in that direction first. He can't get away from you this way, and you can keep him under control until the "buzz" is off.

The best place to keep a horse while ponying is to position his throatlatch near your knee. If he moves too far up, he can shoot off and get around the front and his rope can become entangled in the pony horse's bridle. If he drops too far behind, he can sneak around the back and wrap *you* up. If a horse becomes terribly excited and he's close to your knee, you can take a close hold on him and keep him there until he settles. If he's being ponied too far from your knee, he might bid you a fond farewell and go home alone.

LONGEING

Many performance trainers curse the halter people who longe their horses. They feel that a longed horse constantly has his head tugged on so that, by the time he has something like a hackamore put on him, he's numb and doesn't respond. You *can* get around this situation with certain guidelines.

Don't use such a small circle that you *do* have to tug on your horse constantly, nor such a large one that you have no control. Find something in the middle.

Tom and Brenda Long, California trainers, longe all their halter horses when they're not being ponied. Tom uses a *thin* chain over the nose of the horse, used with the longe line. Why over the top? Because, says Tom, "A horse won't rear if you take ahold of him and the chain is over the nose, but if it's under the chin, he might go up." While a regular sized lead shank chain isn't recommended for constant use because of it's numbing effect, the small chain Tom uses doesn't cause that problem. It's just there to remind the horse that there's someone with an advantage on the other end of the line.

The Longs work their horses on leading and standing up before they longe them, so the horses loosen up during this work. When put on the longe line, if the horse wants to run and buck to get the steam off, they allow it to do so. When a horse is feeling this good, Tom and Brenda feel it's best to allow it to move and, after a couple of laps, it will settle down.

Tom Long longes a yearling colt. He uses a chain over the nose. Notice the loose line. No constant pull is put on the colt.

A non-abrasive surface, such as a sand and shavings mixture, is good for longeing. The Longs do have quite a bit of sand mixed in with the dirt in their longeing arena and, through its deepness, the horses are made to work fairly hard. More is thus accomplished in less time.

When a horse is being longed, it sometimes becomes bored and isn't working as hard as it could, so a change in direction often revives it. The turning also helps the horse exercise more muscles.

When building the gaskin and hip area, Tom Long often uses two lines on a horse. One line comes from the halter to his hands on the "inside" of the circle. The other goes around the offside and lays around the hindquarters well above the hocks —higher if it will stay. By flipping this line, the horse drives his hind end under himself further and works harder. A bitting rig can also be used in this way.

Bar Sprite, a two year old daughter of Bright Chip, kicks up her heels in a free play session. Halter horses need the free play to keep them mentally fresh.

FREE PLAY

While some may scoff at a halter horse's chance to get out and rip and zip and possibly even sneak in the chance to roll, it's not a bad idea! Given the space to do it, a horse loves the chance to occasionally spread out and run without someone holding on to him. Not only does it help him physically, but mentally as well. Halter horses are under a great deal of pressure with the confinement and the rigors of daily work. They need to freshen-up their minds, and being turned loose for awhile is an excellent way to do this.

Some halter trainers turn their horses of comparable age out together for some play. Two or three weanlings, or yearlings, will play together and keep each other going for long periods of time. Weanlings, especially, were most active during early morning and late afternoon or evening hours, when they were with their mothers. This is a good time to turn them out and continue the ritual after they're weaned.

Tim Kane occasionally turns his Appaloosa youngsters out together, and says he's never had an instance of one getting hurt. It also helps, he says, to teach the youngsters manners, they learn just how far they can go without being reprimanded by another horse.

THE TREADMILL

Use of the treadmill is on the increase in the halter horse industry, and it seems to be a wise buy if you can afford one. Yet, as more and more come on the market and into use, the prices do seem to be coming down. And, they seem to be a value at any price when you consider some of the advantages.

Because young horses are working on the straight, flat surface of a treadmill, there is no extreme jar to the outside of the cannon bone that a youngster constantly gets when working a circle.

Horses worked on treadmills work harder than those worked on a flat surface. It is, in reality, a walking-in-place hill climb and maximum effort is put out.

Treadmills can be housed inside a barn and moved when necessary, or can easily be covered up and used outside to provide maximum exercise even during bad weather.

WORKING IN THE ROUND PEN

Nothing gives a person a more powerful feeling than to stand in the center of a round pen and chase a halter horse around with a whip! The control is there. He can't get away from you because he *has* to work that circle. You're not tugging on him because there's nothing on his head. You can turn him into

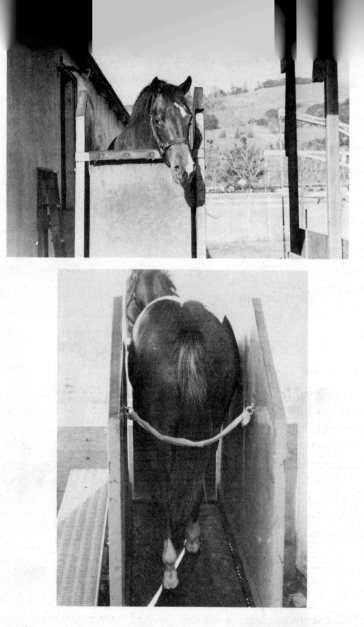

Halcyon Farms swears by the treadmill which keeps their Appaloosa halter horses in excellent condition. Because the horses are working flat, in a straight line, there is no extreme jar to the outside of the cannon bone on growing youngsters.

A youngster can learn his leads working in the round pen.

the fence, which drives him onto his rear end and makes him use those hip and gaskin muscles. He can be worked at the walk, trot or lope.

Only remember that constant circle work is hard on the legs of a growing youngster, which doesn't mean he can't spend *some* time traveling the circle, particularly if the ground is soft and level. Working in this circle also helps him learn his leads and teaches him to arc his body into his direction of travel. Then, when you begin riding him, half the battle is won.

BACKING

This excellent exercise for the hip and gaskin muscles is best done at the end of a session, when the horse has already done some other work and the muscle tissue is broken down. He'll be a little tired and working hard when he's backed, and this will give him the maximum benefit.

The author backs Rodeo Cowboy after each workout. This helps in developing muscle tone in his hip and gaskin area.

When you first begin teaching the horse to back, you may want to place a chain over his nose, and reinforce the action by using a short whip on the front legs or the chest. Push him back and keep him going, preferably in fairly deep ground. Remember that backing gives you maximum effort and tires a horse quickly, so you may have to work to keep him going. The effort is better spent in *constant* backing than it is in backing, then walking forward, then backing again. The stress has to be constant, unbroken work over a long period of time, not a few steps back now and then.

When the horse gets the idea, try to abandon the use of the chain if you can. Keep the "feel" in the horse.

ISOMETRICS

People who are into fitness for themselves know that the fastest way to strengthen the muscles is through isometric

Slapping the horse on the rear end causes him to tighten his hip muscles.

exercise. These include such exercises as pressing your palms against each other while they are held out in front of your chest, and sucking in and holding your stomach muscles tight to the count of ten. So now you say, "Isometrics for horses?"

Why not? During the rainy season, when you're minus a covered area to work your horse, you can at least spend a few minutes in his stall each day working the hip area. Stand your horse against a wall, backed near a corner. Position yourself near his shoulder so you're out of reach if he kicks. Hold his head steady, then pop him just above the tail set with your hand. He's going to tuck under and tighten his hip muscles. Do this repeatedly, but not so much that he becomes used to it and doesn't react.

Another method is to back him slowly into the wall. When he feels it touch him, he's going to tuck under and tighten. Though this method of exercise certainly can't replace outside exercise, it is a way to work on keeping your horse toned when you just can't go outside.

When backed into a wall, a horse will tighten his hip muscles—a form of isometrics. This is usually done in a stall and is particularly helpful during bad weather, when the horse cannot be worked outside.

Hill Work

Ponying a horse up and down hills is an excellent means of exercising him. While you may think he drives hardest off his hind end when climbing a hill, watch him work as he comes *down.* It's just as hard. You can spend half the time working hills as you do working flat, and reap twice the benefits.

Some young horses, especially when growing quickly, will occasionally have a mild tightening of the tendons in the front legs, which causes them temporarily to look as though they're standing over at the knees. This once happened to a daughter of Doc's Blanton just a few short days before the Cow Palace weanling futurity. Nothing was wrong with the filly, outside of that fast growth. No soundness trouble whatsoever. The veterinarian suggested that the filly be ponied up hills to stretch the tendons. It was done, and within three days she was back to normal, standing straight and tall. How did she do at the futurity? Second out of over one hundred!

RIDING

Horses of riding age can naturally be saddled and worked with a rider. So many halter horses also show in performance classes that this is the ideal way to keep them fit for both. There is also something about good, hard work and wet saddle blankets that keeps a horse calm and sensible.

Whatever form of exercise you use, use it daily or every other day, depending on the age and fitness degree of the horse. Increase the work as he can take it and watch for areas that might need more work than others.

WORK BOTH SIDES

Never lose sight of the fact that a horse needs equal work on *both* sides in order to develop all his muscles. Working only one way puts the stress on just one side. If you want him to look great from any angle, give him just as many laps in each direction. Imagine how silly a horse would look with a bulging right forearm and a flat left one! Avoid it. Keep him working in both directions to keep him "equal."

Chapter 7

Working on Problem Areas

Getting a halter horse to its correct weight will be first on your list. Soggy fat has no place on a halter horse. Neither does a prominent set of ribs. You have to decide what's best for your horse as an individual, and put him at that weight. Then you may still have to work to do to improve the throatlatch and neck, the bottom line and, of course, the muscle definition.

Take a look at your horse. Does he need weight added or taken off? His general conformation should help you make the decision. Generally speaking, an extremely short-backed horse looks "piggy" if he's packing too much weight, so this type of horse should be kept a little thinner. Strive for a weight that lets you *feel*, through the skin, the first three ribs, *without seeing them*. Keep him tight and lean.

Is your horse long-backed? If so, he's going to need more weight to fill him up in the flank area and give him the appearance of being somewhat shorter backed. You may run into some trouble here because long-backed horses often are plagued with "droopy" bottom lines, so at the same time you are adding weight to this horse, you will be working him to keep his bottom line from drooping.

If your horse is a little slight in the hip, some added weight may help him look better in this area. The trick is to allow the weight to be distributed where it *should* go, and keep the excess off areas such as that bottom line.

Thinning Down the Obese Horse

As an example of how to thin down a horse that's packing much too much weight, I'll cite the case of a tremendously easy-keeper who was kept a little too well. My own mare, Scamp's Patches, is extremely hard to keep trim. At age two, and a hefty 1050 pounds, it was necessary to trim her down. Dr. Jim Burns, D.V.M., of Sunol, California, was contacted. He ran tests on the mare and diagnosed that an increase in activity, a decrease in feed, and the addition of a thyroid medicine to the feed ration was in order. Scamp's Patches also had a bad bottom line and every effort had to be made to pull it up as much as possible. Since the filly was still growing, she needed proper nutrition in the diet.

Dr. Burns was and still is not convinced that changing a horse from good leafy hay to cubes or pellets will pull up a belly, though some people do believe that. He feels the best feed to combat a belly is Timothy Hay. Since this is extremely hard to find on the West Coast, he gave good, short stemmed leafy alfalfa as his second choice for this filly.

Sweet feed was removed from the diet completely and replaced with hard or crimped oats. Sea Kelp, high in vitamins and extremely good in helping to produce a top hair coat, was added in moderation. Calf Manna, nutritious and especially helpful with growing horses, was put in the ration. Soybean meal, another "plus" in producing a good coat, was prescribed as an addition to the feed. It is high in protein and since the filly would have an increase in activity, she would need this extra protein to carry her through the work.

The complete formulation of hay/grain feeds for weight reduction of this filly was as follows:

HAY

Timothy or Alfalfa Hay: Free choice to total 15 to 20 pounds daily

GRAIN
(total daily, divided into 2 feedings)

Hard or Crimped Oats:	No more than 6 pounds
Calf Manna:	1 pound
Sea Kelp:	½ cup
Soybean Meal:	1 to 2 pounds depending on the amount of work

In addition to this feed, a prescription called *Thyrone* was added to the feed for thyroid function, at the rate of one heaping tablespoon a day for 30 to 60 days. Since this filly was getting fat deposits in the shoulders, withers and neck, this program would be extremely helpful in breaking them down. In about 18 to 21 days, with the use of this medicine, softening of the fat plaques occurred, and they began to seemingly "melt away." After 30 to 40 days, fat was noticeably being worked off, with the horse becoming much more alert and showing a big increase in vigor.

Keep in mind that throughout this program, the filly was being worked almost daily. As her condition improved, the work increased.

ADDING WEIGHT TO THE THIN HORSE

Many problems occur with adding weight too fast, and getting so enthused about the change in the horse that the gaining process isn't halted before the horse becomes *too* heavy. Also, too many people begin a horse on a weight gaining program without looking into the reasons for his being thin to begin with.

If you decide to begin working on a horse that is thin, and you don't know *why* he is thin, it's time to ask your veterinarian. First, take a small manure sample in to the veterinary hospital and ask for a fecal check. Through the microscope, the vet can examine the sample and determine what type of worms the horse has and how heavily he is infested—which could be one cause of his condition. Worming preparations vary, depending on what you're after. In some instances, tube worming might be more effective than paste worming, but you can be sure that if paste will work, your vet will prescribe some and send you home to do your own worming.

Next on the list will be to check the horse's teeth. As an immediate check, you can take hold of the horse's tongue and bring it out the side of the mouth so he can't bite down. Then run your other hand *carefully* up each line of the back teeth, top and bottom, and feel for sharp edges. If he has them, you'll know they're there! This will warrant a "floating" by the veterinarian who can file them down and make it less painful for the horse to eat. The vet can also check to see if the bite is satisfactory and if the horse's teeth line up so he can chew with the greatest efficiency.

If the horse is severely thin and listless, laboratory work with blood samples can be done by your vet to check iron, protein, calcium and phosphorous levels, as well as liver and kidney functions, to name a few. Often, the addition of an oral preparation, such as Lixotinic which adds iron and B vitamins, can build a horse back up to par.

One of the worst things an owner can do is to try to put the weight on a horse overnight. Colic and founder can result from "throwing the feed" to a thin horse that isn't used to it. Increases should be done gradually, spending a few weeks building up the horse's tolerance to this new feeding plan. Yes, it's tempting to throw in much too much grain, and try to get the horse to eat everything right away, but it's dangerous.

Sweet feeds generally contain corn and barley, which are great fatteners. Start the horse on five pounds or less of sweet feed broken up into two or more feedings daily. Increase the amount by a half pound each day until the horse is up to about 15 pounds. The same is true with the amount of hay or pellets. Start small and build up slowly.

Getting a horse to eat isn't a problem if he's naturally a glutton, but some aren't. Often, a horse that is extremely poor, won't eat well. This is particularly evident if a person puts too much feed before the horse and tries free choicing a poor eater. The interest in food seems to diminish even more. If your horse is a poor eater and you're trying to fatten him, try one or more of the following:

Grass   If you have access to fresh green grass, pasture or wild, take the horse out and let him graze for five or ten minutes, then return him to his hay and grain. The grass gets the digestive juices going and seems to perk up the horse's appetite.

Bitters   Go to a liquor store and purchase a bottle of bitters, the type used to mix drinks. These bitters are used in the East to encourage draft horses to eat so their weight can be kept up for pulling competition. Shake out several drops of the bitters on the horse's tongue, two or more times per day, and it will help increase his appetite. Certain brands of bitters have directions on the label for human use in stimulating the appetite. This is no doubt where the idea came about to also use it on livestock.

Open Air   Some horses just brought in from pasture and confined to stalls long to be outside, or in the company of other horses. Often, taking a horse like this out of the stall, tying him to a fence outside and hanging his feed bucket there, will give him the lift he needs to make him start eating.

Small Feedings   Don't feed large amounts. Try feeding the horse three or more times a day, giving him just a little at a time, adding no more until he's cleaned up the previous feeding.

Exercise   Exercise helps the appetite. Sometimes just ponying a horse at a walk for fifteen or twenty minutes helps. If the horse is in good enough condition to take more work (some very poor horses aren't), work him a little harder, cool him out, and feed him *small amounts* an hour or so later.

BAD BOTTOM LINE

Contrary to the poor horse is the one who is a little on the hefty side, many of which have saggy bottom lines. A bad bottom line, however, isn't *always* on a heavy horse. Some horses can be worked seemingly to death, and when they stand around, the belly relaxes and "hangs loose." If it's a conformation fault, you can limit it but not make it disappear. If it's just a case of too much food and not enough exercise, you can fight it successfully—but it can be quite a battle. Yet, in some cases, a feed change helps tremendously.

While Dr. Burns, who prescribed the slimming program for the overweight filly, does not feel pellets and cubes always pull off a belly, he *does* swear by Timothy Hay, which is excellent, if you can get it. Some people do swear by the use of cubes and pellets, abandoning hay. The only thing you can do is to experiment with your own horse and see which works best for him. One thing that *may* help, if perhaps he's getting pellets and hay along with his grain, is to switch your feeding around before a show.

To suck up the bottom line before a show, take away the horse's hay about four days prior to his class. Keep him only on his grain and pellets or cubes. His belly should draw up and look tight by the time of the show.

Working naturally helps remove some of the belly on horses with bad bottom lines. This is disgusting to certain owners, because horses with good bottom lines, when worked, suck up straight and beautifully, yet the horse with the bad bottom line works just as hard and looks great while working, but bellied-up while relaxing. What do you do in this case?

First, try some galloping and also some backing for exercise that is tough on those bellies. If it's not doing the trick, you'll have to use some show ring strategy. As you undoubtedly notice, when the horse is tense the belly comes up tight. The trick is to keep your horse on the muscle while in the show

Poking the belly will cause the horse to "suck it up."

ring. If for some reason you can't keep him on his toes, spend a few moments before the class poking him low on one side of the barrel. He'll get a little tender there. Before the judge gets to you—just before—sneak back and poke the colt there again . . . and he'll suck up the belly. This type of "tummy poking" may also be done at home, working something like the isometrics explained in the exercise chapter. Each time you poke the horse, he'll tighten and hold the muscles, which will strengthen them.

Trimming the Neck

No matter how nice a neck and throatlatch a horse has, you can always make it *just that much nicer* through sweating and the use of neck wraps. If your horse's neck is much too large because of too much weight, you need to slim him down *and* to sweat his neck. In both cases (the good neck and the bad), sweating helps tremendously.

Liquid glycerine is excellent for producing a good sweat on a horse, and keeping it going if the area is covered. Neoprene neck wraps, with Velcro fasteners, are available through most tack shops. As a matter of personal preference, I use one ten-inch-wide throatlatch wrap first. Over it goes the full neck sweat, and then another thinner throatlatch wrap is put over that, both to keep it fastened and to add more warmth to the throatlatch. Before these are put on, glycerine is rubbed all around the throatlatch area and the neck. If the horse is a little cresty in the mane area, particular attention should be given to making sure it is well saturated with glycerine.

There are some people who mix a "magic formula" of several different ingredients to sweat necks. In most cases, it has been passed down from person to person, and by the time it gets down the line, nobody really knows why each ingredient was added. Some of these "miracle preparations" have been known to blister a horse. For this reason, I highly recommend using only straight glycerine for sweating, because it is safe and mild. It can be purchased from any druggist and, incidentally, is more economical when purchased in larger quantities.

When you work a horse with the sweat hood, if he's worked quite long when he's just beginning a fitness program, he'll begin a lathery sweat. What you're after is that eventual clear, drippy sweat. Work the horse into the sweat, then walk him until his pulse and respiration have dropped back down to normal. By that time, it is safe to tie him somewhere and let him drip. The longer and more consistently you use this sweat gear, the better neck you'll produce.

Tie the horse away from drafts and out of the sun. It's best to cross-tie him, so he can't rub—and he *will* want to rub because dripping sweat is irritating.

To sweat a neck, first apply a ten-inch throatlatch wrap.

Next, apply the full neck sweat.

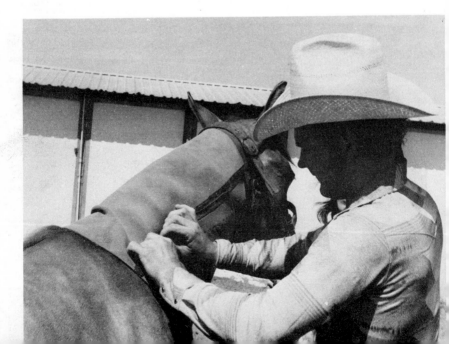

If the full sweat tends to come undone, put another throatlatch wrap over it.

Work the horse, and let him continue to sweat.

The duration of the sweating process can last any period from twenty minutes to two hours, depending on how much you need to take off the neck.

When the horse is done, remove the sweat gear and rinse the neck and throatlatch area thoroughly. Be especially careful to remove all traces of glycerine and sweat from the mane area, or the horse will begin rubbing and rub out his mane.

Once you've gone through the rigors of sweating down a neck, you'll work harder to prevent it from getting chunky. Remember that those fattening feeds, such as barley and corn, always seem to add fat to the neck and shoulders, especially with stud colts. Some horses have to be slimmed *way* down, and sweated, in order to regain a good neck after a bout with obesity.

Neck wraps, left on while the horse is in the stall, work much the same as a ring does, restricting the size of the finger underneath.

Neck collars left on while the horse is in the stall help in giving definition and trimness to the throatlatch. They come in several materials, ranging from felt to leather with sheep-wool lining (possibly the best type of neck collar). Neoprene sweat-type wraps shouldn't be left on as the skin becomes too moist and will macerate.

The collars are to be put on quite snugly. They don't sweat a neck, but rather work in the way that a ring on your finger does. It it's a little small for you, it makes your finger smaller under it. The same is true of the neck collar. Put the collar on snugly and leave it there, except for the times the horse is being worked, groomed or washed.

Mutton Withers

Mutton withers are looked down on by judges. If a horse does not naturally have super wither definition, and he's up in weight and fit for halter, he may look somewhat mutton withered. This is true often with young horses, such as yearlings and two-year-olds. With the older horses, withers seem to define when the animal is ridden, and the saddle's presence works them up. With younger colts and fillies, you may want to put a light saddle on and longe, pony or otherwise work them saddled. In extreme cases, you can rub the withers with glycerine and lay a neck sweat or piece of plastic sheeting over the withers, under the saddle, while you longe or pony the horse, or put him on the walker. Be careful of irritation, but you shouldn't have much trouble if the saddle is lightweight and fits properly.

Improving Muscle Definition

By reviewing the exercise chapter, you can select one or more exercises that will help strengthen your horse's weaker points.

If he needs increased muscle tone in his hips, back him. This will help the hip and gaskins. If his forearm and shoulder area need work, move him forward at the long trot. Each exercise helps for overall fitness, but some work harder on certain areas.

Just remember that you can't produce what the horse doesn't have. If he's flat muscled and small, you can't make a bulging muscleman out of him. While you can reduce a neck and "clean it up" if it's short and stubby, you can't change its length. Work to improve your horse all you can . . . and then go for it!

Chapter 8

Coat Care and Grooming

"Yes, good feed makes the hair coat better, but what makes it even better than that is the daily grooming. There's no short-cut to the rubbing and grooming. If you put two horses side by side and they've been fed the same feed, but one has been groomed regularly, the one with the grooming will have the best hair coat."

The man who made this statement, in front of three thousand horsemen at the California Livestock Symposium, should certainly know what produces a good coat, for the horses he shows are the ultimate in halter horses. His name is Tommy Manion and, as of the 1978 Symposium, this man had shown sixteen World Champions at the World Championship Quarter Horse Shows. At the All American Quarter Horse Congress, he's had a winner in one of its halter futurities for nine straight years.

Tommy Manion knows the value of grooming, both as a trainer and as one of the nation's most respected judges. You just can't take a halter horse into the ring without having given him every possible advantage to cop a shot at a win. For this reason, I interviewed a great many trainers and exhibitors and came up with some solid guidelines for producing a fine hair coat.

109

Jerry Wells scores a big win with a perfectly groomed Quarter Horse gelding. Daily grooming pays off!

How to Groom

What you use to groom your halter horse has a lot to do with your success in getting a shiny, natural looking coat. Plastic devices, shedding blades and even some harsh rubber curry combs can break off the hair and give it an irregular, clipped look. The brush boxes of many top halter horse fitters today hold a rubber grooming mitt, a stiff brush, a soft body brush and rub rags (Irish linen is tops here).

To replace many harsh grooming devices, trainers have gone to rubber mitts. A mitt fits well on your hand and is so flexible you can use it to wrap around and brush such hard to groom places as the inside gaskin and forearm. The mitt is gentle enough to use on a horse's face to remove shedding hair, and can be used below the knees and hocks, unlike some other grooming tools. It's a super, overall grooming tool; and when accompanied by brushing and rubbing with rags, the effectiveness is maximum.

To be truly effective, grooming should be done twice daily. You'll find each session will be thirty minutes or longer, if you do things the way they *should* be done. The more you put into it, the more you get out!

One of the best times to do the "before workout" grooming is first thing in the morning. When a horse is bundled up all night in warm blankets and a hood, he's warm clear through. The shedding hair is loosened, so now it works off easily. Throughout the night, the friction of the blankets has worked to loosen other hair, so now your brush takes that off too, and more.

Keep your horse out of cold air and drafts when you pull the blankets to groom him. When cold air hits the hair coat, it can retard shedding and set you back as much as two weeks in your quest to produce a short coat. When you remove blankets in the morning, if it's brisk, try to do your grooming under a heat lamp. If it's extremely cold, you'll probably have to sacrifice

Joanie Cohn uses a rubber grooming mitt on Hug N Tuff.

the daily grooming ritual and just leave the blankets on for the day.

It's best to cross tie your horse for grooming, as this gives you equal access to each side and more room for working. Cross ties can easily be set up in a stall or alleyway. If you can afford the luxury, it's nice to have a special grooming stall, with a wood, concrete or rubber matted floor, where you can put a heat lamp and can have storage areas for all your grooming tools. Such a stall, equipped with a floor drain, can also serve as an indoor wash rack.

Where you groom your horse doesn't matter as much as being thorough. When you start your grooming with the rubber mitt, begin by using it very gently on the forehead area to loosen the hair on the head, above the eyes, and on the jowls. If your horse is spooky about having his head handled, it's best to untie him when you work on it, so you don't risk the problem of having him pull back on the cross ties.

Once you've loosened the dirt and hair around the face, go down the side of the neck. Following the lay of the hair, use long, firm strokes and lean into it! Work one side of the horse at a time and concentrate on one area, doing it thoroughly, rather than skipping around and missing some places.

After you've done the entire neck, start down the top line. Work from the withers back to the croup, then down to the base of the tail, paying particular attention to the crop area which seems to be a gathering place for dust and debris. When the top of the back is done, start on the shoulder and groom it thoroughly. Next, work the side of the barrel to the flanks, then do the top and side of the hip.

Don't forget the bottom half of the barrel and the belly area. All too often, people skip grooming this section because it's hard to reach. Nothing looks worse than a slick horse with a fuzzy belly! It not only detracts from the overall appearance of the coat, but if the hair is not smoothed down on the belly, the horse's bottom line loses smoothness.

The inside and outside of the forearm and gaskin can't be overlooked either. Wrap your mitt around the curves and vigorously work downward. You can also use the mitt to work down to the coronary band from the forearms and gaskins.

When you've covered virtually every inch of one side of your horse, do the same on the other side. When working on the mane side, be sure to get under the mane and groom that section of the neck well. (See instructions for care of the mane and tail in Chapter Ten.)

Stiff body brushes will work to further loosen dirt and loose hair. This type of brush should be used directly following the use of the rubber mitt. Wrist action is extremely important in the use of this brush. By getting in deep and flicking the brush at the end of the stroke, you actually throw the loose hair and debris off the coat, rather than just depositing it elsewhere. Use the stiff brush and follow the same pattern as you did with

Tim Kane uses the stiff and soft body brushes on Quinta's King.

the rubber mitt, but because of the harshness of this brush don't use it around the face or below the knees and hocks.

A soft body brush is used after the stiff brush to lay down and polish the hair. This brush *is* soft enough to use on the face and other tender areas. The soft brush should be used all over the horse with sweeping strokes, and flicked at the end of each.

Rub rags give the finishing touch. This final rubbing does a great job of laying the hair down absolutely flat, and seems to help the natural oils, which have been brought up by brushing, to blend with the hair. If you're fighting a bad coat, you might put a small amount of baby oil on the rag and rub the entire coat with it. You can also do this in the area of the face, and use the baby oil or mineral oil on the rag to clean out the nostrils and remove scale from the inside of the ears. Remember to have enough rags on hand so that you always have a clean one to use.

If you have been going through all the rigors of trying to produce a top coat and are not getting results, you may wish to consult your veterinarian. Poor coat condition is sometimes a signal of disease. Also, most halter horses are on a high-protein diet. If the diet is high in protein but deficient in energy, a horse can develop a dry coat, for the protein needed for the hair shafts is often used instead to provide necessary energy. If you are frustrated by a lot of work and a coat that's not improving, by all means talk to your veterinarian.

Chances are, however, that producing a top coat is just a matter of time, and all of us are impatient about getting results. We can't wait to get the fitness and shine on that horse and get him to the show ring. We want him to sparkle. Yet, you might be setting the coat back by giving him that good "before work" grooming, but cheating on the second one—after exercise.

After a horse has been worked, his pores are open and the natural oils are just waiting for a chance to be brought to the surface. All too often, a person is as tired as the horse after a workout in the pen, or on the longe line, or with a pony horse. Maybe you decide to skip the clean-up of the horse "just this once," then it becomes a habit. Stop and think. Especially if you were using a sweat hood, your horse worked up a good sweat while you were exercising him. All the dust he kicked up is stuck onto the sweat, and the salt that is in the sweat makes the mess even worse. It all gangs up on the hair coat and, if it is left there, it dries out the hair and robs you of that shiny coat you want so much.

Whenever weather permits, rinse the horse off after a workout. Use warm water. If you don't have a hose that hooks up to a hot and cold water tap, you can purchase a small, electrical, water heater which you merely plug in to a standard outlet. The heating device is set into a large bucket, or trash can, of water. When you're done working the horse, you can sponge the grime off his coat. Some trainers add small amounts of

When weather permits, rinse the horse off after a workout.

vinegar or alcohol to the rinse to help even more in removing salty sweat and grime.

Daily rinsing doesn't remove the natural oils if the water is *lukewarm*. Cold water doesn't do the job in getting the coat clean and hot water does strip the oils. Warm water is the only temperature that is conducive to producing a clean, shiny coat.

Sometimes the weather is too brisk to make it wise to rinse the coat, but that's still no excuse for not cleaning your horse. Whether he's been sponged off with warm water, or is sweaty and is going to dry naturally before you brush the grime out of him, tie him in the shade. "Hang him out to dry" in a barn alleyway, under a tree, or cross tie him in his stall . . . as long as you avoid drafts, and keep the sun off his back. And, washed or not, the horse still needs that good after-workout grooming.

You're just way ahead of the game if you were able to rinse the grime from his coat.

When the horse is dry, repeat the entire process you used in the morning grooming. Put your heart into it, because the pores are open now and you're going to notice the natural oils coming to the surface. The results will be gratifying.

Vacuuming a horse is a good way to remove debris from the coat, but it is certainly no substitute for grooming. Like rinsing a horse, a good vacuuming removes the bulk of the grime, allowing you to get more out of your grooming. If you're going to a show and for some reason you can't, or don't want to, wash your horse before it, you can probably get a spit-polish shine by vacuuming him well, washing only his white markings, and grooming heavily.

Clean stalls mean clean horses! Whether you bed with straw or shavings, bed deeply enough so the horse isn't skinning his hocks constantly on the flooring and so the dampness can seep down from the top layer and the horse isn't laying in damp bedding all the time. Improperly bedded, unkept stalls are also responsible for staining the knees and hocks of white-legged horses, such as Paints. If you own a light-coated horse, you know how hard it is to keep him stain free even when you're cleaning his stall regularly. He'll always find "that spot" to lay in and get that stain. If you do clean your stall daily, you minimize the problem. Keeping a large bushel basket by the stall door will allow you, each time you have a few moments to go in, to pick up droppings and remove wet spots from the bedding. If you do this daily, your bedding will last longer, which is definitely economical, and your horse will stay nicer.

If for some reason your white-legged horse doesn't agree and keeps managing to stain his knees and hocks, it only takes a few minutes each day to wet them down and scrub the stains with a horse shampoo and a small fingernail brush. Rinse it clean and you've removed a stain which, if left on for any length of time, might be extremely hard to get off before a show.

Bathing

What if the horse must be bathed completely. Perhaps he was let out to play and he rolled, or maybe he's just due for a bath. There are a great many halter horse fitters who avoid bathing a horse at all costs for fear of stripping the coat of oils and dulling it. Just as many trainers take the other view and argue that frequent bathing doesn't damage the coat. This is definitely my own stand. Look at the facts.

Horse shampoos on the market today, such as Orvus, are especially made to "lock in" natural oils. Using lukewarm water, you clean the horse, but don't strip the oil. You are getting damaging, dulling grime out of the coat, and preventing coat problems. If you wash your horse thoroughly, then blanket him after he's dry, his hair is going to lay down and retain its shine.

There is a theory that if you wash a horse, it must be at least two days prior to a show for his coat to look good by show time. Here again, you must study the facts. Halter horses are in top health. They're fit. A fit horse wants to work. If you wash your horse that far in advance of a show, about the only way you're going to keep him clean is to leave him in his stall. If he's a "high" colt, you almost *have* to work him good the day or two before the show so he won't give you trouble in the halter ring. Try working him well the morning before the show, then wash him early in the afternoon, while he's satisfied from the workout and is content to stay in the stall.

Last minute washing is often necessary, particularly if you're at a multiple judge show where halter and performance classes are repeated over two or more days. At the Bakersfield, California Fall Paint Show and Futurities, when showing a weanling futurity colt one year, I saw many halter horse exhibitors washing their horses at four or five o'clock in the morning, just a few hours before the classes. They'd walk the horses dry, cover them up until class time, and the horses looked super.

This has become a common practice at shows such as this.

Whenever your horse is wet from a bath, take the opportunity to work at removing the chestnuts from his legs, both front and hind. When wet, the chestnuts become soft and you can peel them off a little at a time until they lay flat at the same level as the rest of the skin on the leg. You can also soften them with oil.

The ergots, small bony growths on the back of the fetlocks, should also be removed if you expect a smooth look in this area after you clip the horse. These growths can be twisted off when wet, or oiled and worked off. Hoof nippers can also be used, as long as you are careful and don't cut in too far.

Waiting "in the wings" just before the Cow Palace weanling futurity, this youngster wears the nylon lined blanket and hood that has kept her coat short, shiny, and "futurity ready."

BLANKETING

Blanketing is a big expense, but it's essential for the conditioning of a halter horse. In order to keep the horse clean, and for the body temperature to be regulated and the warmth held, blankets and sheets have to be used. When a horse is kept warm, his hair lays down and stays in better condition. The warmth and rubbing action of the blankets, while the horse moves, promotes shedding. You can even prevent, or postpone, a winter coat by properly blanketing a halter horse.

Blankets help maintain the horse's body temperature at a more constant level. If it's a colder day than normal, you can add an extra blanket and keep the horse as warm as he was the day before. Change in temperature just naturally affects the haircoat. And, while daily grooming is a must, sometimes it should be a *must not*. If you pull blankets on an extremely cold day, the chilly air fuzzes up the coat and can retard shedding.

What kind of blanket should you use? Styles and fads have changed over the years, but the current trend seems to be the wisest of all. Common in the past were fleece- and flannel-lined blankets which seemed to keep the horse fairly warm. They caused havoc, however, when a horse began to shed. Loose hair would ball up in the lining, causing the horse to rub and itch. Naturally, hoods were rubbed off constantly, and walked on as they lay on the stall floor. Many horses became escape artists and could easily scoot a blanket right over the head and onto the floor, surcingles buckled and intact. Most trainers feel that at least 75 per cent of the rubbing problem is caused by hair accumulating in the blanket lining, causing the horse to itch badly. Some trainers have seen horses become so frantic for relief, that they become cast in the stall when they lay down and attempt to roll the itch away.

Relief has come, both for itchy, shedding horses and the poor owners who used to clog up washing machines with hair from fleece and flannel blankets during laundering. The newer

*Blanketing helps fight off winter coats, as evidenced by this slick
daughter of Rooster Cogburn.*

blankets and hoods are completely lined with nylon, satin, or other "slippery" type inner-linings which produce a better coat than blankets of the past. Hair is rubbed loose, then released to fall. Nothing clings to the lining, the blankets stay cleaner and the horses get relief from itching.

Kenny Campbell, a halter fitter from Aubrey, Texas, looked at the nylon-lined blankets for the first time and thought he'd find them on the floor by morning, because they'd slither off the horses! To his surprise, they stayed put, because the horses had no real desire to get them off. If a horse should roll in a blanket during everyday use, these newer blankets are equipped with butt straps, or straps which go around the back legs, and they stay in place. Kenny Campbell now uses these exclusively.

The nylon-lined blankets are generally washable in cool water. Keep them clean and never put a soiled blanket on a clean horse. Also, be sure your blankets fit the horse properly. You want as much of him covered up as possible. If a blanket is too small, a horse's hip and croup area can be exposed, as well as part of his barrel. You'll find that the higher priced blankets generally run more true to size than the cheaper ones. When you buy a certain size in a good blanket, you know it will *be* that size. Good blankets will also outlast several of the cheap ones, and they're usually cut to an extremely good fit. Cheap blankets often aren't contoured correctly.

The blanket your halter horse wears should have an extra deep cutback at the withers to protect manes, so the hair on the withers doesn't "crunch up" or rub out. You need maximum coverage to retain body heat and to keep the coat short and clean all over. Because the bottom line, the forearm and the gaskin are critically judged areas in a show, they should be treated accordingly. A blanket should come down far enough that these areas aren't exposed. While most blankets won't go under to cover the entire belly, a good one, well cut, will reach under quite a bit, smoothing the hair and helping the horse shed out in this area—seemingly the last place winter hair breaks loose.

Your blanket should either overlap well at the chest closure, or should be a reinforced and closed front: the type that is slipped over the head rather than buckled in front. This allows for comfortable fit and keeps that all-important chest area covered.

The newer blankets have higher fronts that come way up on the horse's shoulder and fit higher at the chest. When combined with a hood, there is no gap in the coverage of these areas. A good blanket will also wrap around the tail area, and will have dee rings to allow for a butt strap to keep the blanket in place.

Hoods keep the hair coat slick on the head and neck and keep the mane laying flat. Nothing tames a mane like a well fitted hood. Conventional hoods always had a small satin-type lining in the mane area, but the same problems existed as long as the rest of the inside hood was flannel- or fleece-lined. The horse would rub to try to remove it. Halter horse fitters now seem to be changing over to hoods which, like the new blankets, are completely lined with a nylon or satin type material.

Hood connector straps, which keep hoods in place by holding them to the blanket, don't seem to be made for horses: they often "pop" if the horse finds some reason to rub the hood against the stall wall or feeder. Dee rings should be on the *side* of the hood, connected to the *side* of the blanket. If they're on top, the elastic strap will pinch at the wither area and rub out some of the mane. There is less security with a top strap than there is with two side straps. If you have extreme problems in keeping a hood on your escape artist, try different ways to rig up the connectors.

If the hood has a dee ring, take a small loop of baling wire, form a loop through the ring and twist it off, with several smooth wraps, so there is no sharp edge and the loop is secure. Put another loop of the same type on the dee ring of the blanket. Join them together with baling twine or a heavy strip of elastic. This is much stronger than one long elastic fastener.

Bungee cords (elastic tie down cords) can be rigged with swivel snaps and used as hood connectors. In extreme cases of "hood escape," you can sew a dee ring to the blanket front and another to the bottom end of the hood and connect the hood to the blanket in front and on both sides. Once a horse finds out it's no longer easy to slip out of the hood, we can only hope he will stop trying.

Another method of keeping a horse from slipping a hood over his head is to have some sort of strap around his neck, at the throatlatch area, which fits snugly enough so that the hood can't be slipped off. You can make one from an old piece of blanket surcingle strap and blanket hardware. An old belt or bridle throatlatch strap can also be used. Some hoods come with the surcingle-type strap sewn in.

During summer months, when it's too hot to keep heavy blankets on a horse, a lightweight sheet takes the place of a blanket in keeping the hair lying down flat, and keeping the hair coat clean. Many of the newer sheets are a mesh-type material which can be worn even on the hottest days. It's also nice to have an extremely lightweight sheet to put on your horse when you work him to keep the bright sun from burning his coat.

Yes, the sun *will* burn a coat, especially during the hottest part of the day, but this doesn't mean that your horse has to spend his life in a cave. If he's out in the pasture all day, naturally his coat is going to sun burn. If he's sweaty from exercise, then tied out in the sun to dry, the rays will hit the grime and sweat and dry out his coat. If he's bathed and "hung out to dry" in the sun, he'll no doubt frizz up some. But, because being outside is essential to the growth of the foal, weanling or yearling, sometimes you have to sacrifice one thing for another and allow these babies to spend some time outside, uncovered. Keep in mind that growing horses get their Vitamin D from the sun and that they need about three hours or more of it daily to soak up their requirement. By turning a young horse out, or working him uncovered, before noon or after 4:00 P.M. in the late spring or summer, he can get the benefit of the Vitamin D and avoid the hottest part of the day to keep his nice coat.

Sometimes, a little time out in the sun will promote shedding of the winter coat. The warmth of the sun seems to cause the long hair to break loose. When the hair *is* this long, while the horse is in his winter coat, little damage can be done to the hair coat, as far as sunburning.

Blanketing naturally helps shedding out. Heat lamps in stalls also keep the temperature up, helping the hair coat to break loose. Another method of "tricking" horses into shedding early is to use light in the same way breeders do to get mares to cycle early in the year, before the normal strong heat cycles usually occur. The light method consists of using a 300 watt bulb mounted in the ceiling of the stall. This bulb is left on from 5:00 A.M. until 10:00 P.M. daily, simulating a late spring or summer day.

Halter horse fitters in Central and Northern California have been lucky to have a local tack shop with some imagination! The owner came up with the idea of "horse raincoats," made of raincoat-type plastic material, which fit a horse like a normal blanket, with a couple of exceptions. An additional section is pulled up under the belly to cover it completely. The front wraps around to cover the entire chest with no openings and come up high on the shoulders. The chest and belly sections close with adjustable Velcro. At the same time the raincoat is being used, regular neck sweats can also be put on the horse and he's well covered. This type of "sweat suit" helps trainers shed horses out fast.

The horse is worked with the suit and sweat hoods on. After work, when he's warm but not lathering and puffing, the horse is walked until he's cool enough to be safely cross tied but still warm and damp under the suit. Cross tied, so he can't rub against a wall and roll the sweat gear, the horse is left for

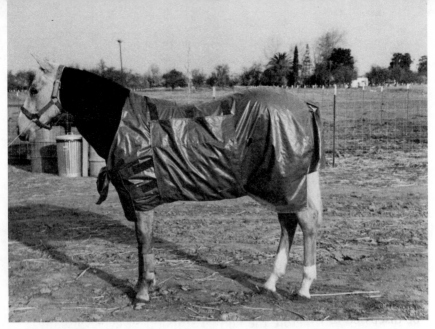

Body suits help produce warmth to stimulate shedding. Notice how this suit comes up under the belly and a front panel wraps completely around the chest to seal the horse in well.

Worked first with a body suit, the horse is then groomed while the hair is "just waiting" to come off.

twenty minutes to an hour. The increased body heat encourages the hair to break loose. As soon as the body suit is removed, heavy grooming should be done, very vigorously, to remove the loosened hair. When you're working on shedding a coat, try to avoid the use of sharp shedding blades which will often break the hair off and give it a clipped or dead appearance. Use a rubber mitt, or even a rubber surgical glove. A pumice-type block will also pull off hair. You can purchase a large block in restaurant supply stores, since it is usually used for cleaning pots and pans. By cutting off small pieces of the block, you have a shedding tool that is economical and easy to use.

Many people resort to body clipping as a means of getting a short coat fast. There are pros and cons to clipping, and they'll be discussed in Chapter Nine. Just remember that clipping can *shorten* a coat, but cannot *improve* it. A shiny coat is the result of good feed, proper parasite control, cleanliness and extensive grooming.

Chapter 9

Clipping and Trimming the Halter Horse

A halter horse can't possibly be judged to the best advantage if a poor clipping job detracts from his conformation and gives an unprofessional appearance. In order for a judge to see those pert, well-shaped ears, they must be cleaned out with the clippers and properly edged. The jaw and jowl areas must be clean and the muzzle well shaven. The length of the bridle path can "make or break" the appearance of the neck. Clipping a halter horse is an art in itself and cannot be done carelessly.

The best clipper to use for general clipping is one of the smaller types—the Oster A-2 or A-5 models, or something comparable. In order to provide detailed instruction on how to clip, it is necessary to refer to exact blade sizes, as different blades give different cuts and you can't properly clip a horse from top to bottom with just one blade. The blades referred to in this chapter are sizes used with Oster clippers.

The most advantageous blades to use are the size 40, a surgical blade, and the size 10, not so deep a cut. A size 30 is also handy and would be used occasionally in the same places as a 10, when a little closer cut is needed, but not so close a cut as the 40 blade would give. These three blades are listed in catalogs, where they can be ordered if you cannot find them at tack shops or pet grooming stores, as follows:

Oster size 10 blade — All Purpose
Oster size 30 blade — Close
Oster size 40 blade — Surgical

Let's examine the different blades, as they are used on various parts of the body. As you can see, the 40 blade gets the most use:

Area to be Clipped	Blade Used
Muzzle	40
Inside nostrils	40
Under jaw and throatlatch	40
Around eyes	40
Ears	40
Bridle path	40
Pastern, fetlock and cannon bone	10 or 30
Body clipping:	
Head and legs	10
General body and neck areas	Use large clipper, such as Sunbeam Clipmaster

When using the size 40 blade, you must learn to angle the clipper. When doing the muzzle area, hold the blade down closer to the skin, so that they will cut all the way down to nip off the nubs. When you get up closer to the top of the mouth, where there is more face hair, don't clip as deeply, as you'll be cutting hair coat and not "whiskers." When you're working around the eyes, don't dig in as much with the clippers, for you only want to remove the guard hairs not the actual coat hair. When doing the bridle path, angle the blade so you get a very close cut but not a "bald" look. Experimenting in between shows will allow you to learn how to angle the clippers properly. Without a show near, if you make mistakes while practicing clipping, the mistakes can grow out before showtime.

WHEN TO CLIP

The best time to use the size 40 blades is two days prior to a show. Do the face, ears and bridle path at this time. The blades will cut short and clean and by the time of the show, you have two day's growth and a natural look, not one of freshly stripped hair. Your horse will be beautifully clipped, but won't look overdone. If you need touch-up work on the nubs of the nose, which grow out quickly on some horses, you can clip them again the morning of the show, or use a hand razor to shave them off shortly before a class.

Since you're not cutting as deeply on the legs, with the size 10 blade, you can do those the day before the show. *Never* use the size 40 blades on the legs, particularly with a white-legged horse, or you'll have a "bald eagle" on your hands. In the case of closely shaven white legs, they'll look pink, from the skin underneath showing through.

USING YOUR CLIPPERS

You can "feather and blend" easily with your clippers. By turning them over and clipping with the clipper upside down, they will only clip half as deeply as when they're in normal position. When you're blending clipped and unclipped areas, such as booting a leg up to the knee, you need to feather and blend, so you don't have a definite line between the clipped and unclipped hair.

Don't grip the clippers tightly. If you do hold them with a "death grip," they'll dig into the hair. Learn to hold and use the clippers properly. Practice holding them lightly and letting them ride easily in your hand. If your horse is clean and his hair is not caked with dirt, a light hold on the clippers will produce a beautiful cut.

Only clip the side at which you're standing. Clip only the part of that side that you can see clearly. Adjust your stance as you clip. Do one side of the muzzle, for example, then walk to the front for the front part, and around to the other side to complete the clipping. Don't just reach around and blindly clip or you'll make mistakes. When you're doing the legs, if you're doing the outside of the left cannon bone (from the left side of the horse) you can do a fine job. While you're at that side, you will have a clear view of the left (inside) of the right leg and you can also clip that. To do the right sides of both legs, go to the right side of the horse.

Keep your clipper blades well lubricated. Most clippers come with instructions that tell you what kind of solution to mix to dip the running blades into for oiling. Sprays, such as Oster Kool Lube, are also available. A standard around most garages and workshops, WD-40 spray, can also be used. Spray or dip your clippers often while using them.

Never use an overheated clipper. It will result in unsightly clipper marks. Booting a horse, clipping the legs all the way up to or above the knees, is a tedious job for any clipper. When you get to the last leg, or last two, you may find the clippers heating and not doing as nice a job. Let them cool *completely* before tackling any more clipper work or you'll have quite a mess. I sometimes boot the front legs of a horse one day and the back legs the next, thus avoiding the temptation to do the job all at once with hot clippers, just to get it done.

CLIPPING THE MUZZLE

Stop to think that a horse's nose is a very sensitive area. Especially if he's never been clipped before, if you shove the clippers toward his muzzle, the horse may think you're going to push them in his mouth. Or, he may panic at the sudden feel of something vibrating against him.

Reassure your horse each time you clip. With one hand, begin rubbing his nose gently with the back of your hand, so he becomes accustomed to something touching him there. At the

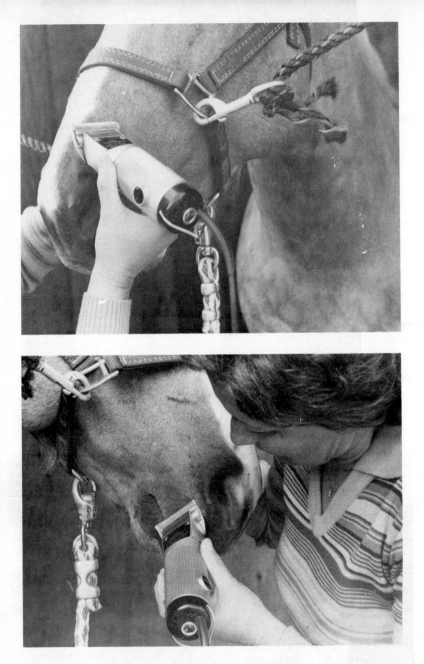

When clipping the muzzle area, clip above the nostril, on the sides, in front, and behind the chin.

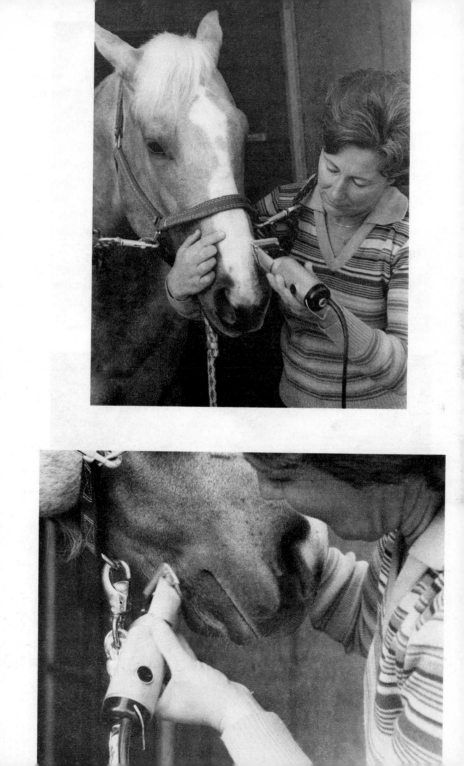

same time, hold the clippers in the other hand and let them run a little way away from him, to get him used to the noise.

When doing the nubs on the muzzle, you want to angle the clippers to cut closely, but you should be extremely light with the clipper. Just come by and barely brush off the nose hairs. If you dig in, particularly at the side of the mouth, you'll make a bad mark and once it's there, it's there until the coat hairs grow out. You don't have to worry about this on the front of the nose as much as you do on the sides. Just remember to be very, very light with the clippers.

The fine, fine hairs inside the nostrils must also be cleaned out, much in the same way as you strip the insides of the ears. And, as with the ears, this is a *very* tender area. Avoid cutting

When clipping the fine hairs inside the nostril, use your thumb to open up and expose the inside area. The horse can easily be hurt by the clippers if he moves, so it's best to restrain him.

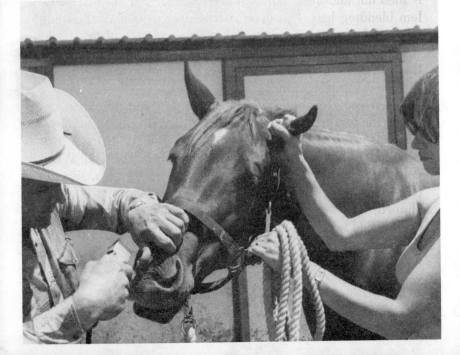

the horse with the clippers as, once you've hurt him, he'll fight you each time you attempt to clip that area. If you think the horse will give you trouble when you try to clip inside his nostrils, restrain him. Have someone hold an ear, or put on a lip cord. (Proper use of restraints is explained in detail later in this chapter.) While the horse is being held still, you can gently fold out the nostril to clip inside.

CLIPPING THE THROATLATCH

On a horse with a very short, fine hair coat, you may have no need to clip the throatlatch area. However, if you have a Paint, Pinto, or a horse with very light hair in that area, you may find that the white hair is denser than the dark. You may want to hold the horse's head up and out and smooth out the hair on the bottom of the throatlatch to enhance the shape.

Clipping under the jaw is done with the size 40 blade. Remember that this blade cuts extremely close, but if your horse is shed out and has a fine hair coat, you should have no problem blending hair. However, if it is *not* completely shed out, you will have to do a great deal of feathering to blend.

Before working in the jaw area, either loosen the halter to the last notch to give you working room underneath, or take it off and secure it around the horse's neck.

When you begin under the horse's chin and jaw area, between the two jaw bones, work up and down with the clippers. There is no need to worry about blending here, because this is an indentation that can't be seen much from the side. When you *do* begin working more to the side of this area, flip the clippers over and begin blending the clipped hair with the unclipped, by feathering with the clipper reversed. You can go up the side normally, if you hold the clippers at a slant with the blade up (so that it does not cut as deeply), but working with a reversed clipper, or a combination of regular and reversed, will give you the nicest look.

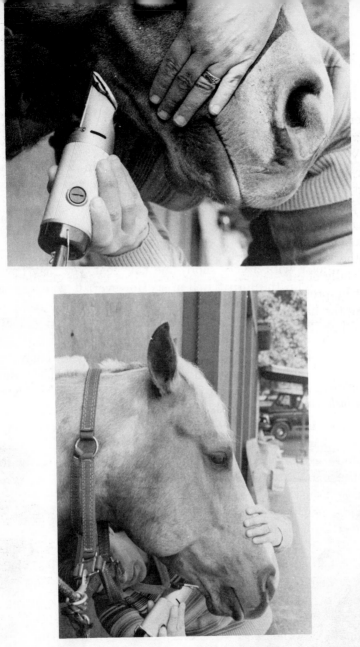

Work both up and down, to feather and blend the hair under the jaw.

CLIPPING AROUND THE EYES

When working around the eyes, remember that you are doing an area that can easily be damaged, so take care and be gentle. What you are after here are the guard lashes, much the same texture as the nose whiskers. You'll want to whisk these off and not cut in as deeply as you did on the muzzle, for the guard lashes protrude from an area which has natural coat hair and a deep cut with the clipper will strip all that natural hair and leave a bald spot.

Another worry, while working in this area, is that you might accidentally clip off the actual eyelashes. This can be guarded against by protecting them with your non-clipper hand. When clipping the hairs of the upper eyelid, gently close the horse's eye and hold it closed with your thumb, which should be posi-

When clipping the guard hairs above the eye, place your thumb over the lashes and hold the eye closed.

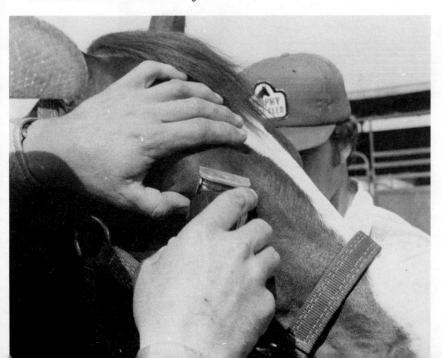

tioned over the natural eyelashes. Clip the upper guard hairs. If your thumb is directly covering the lash, you have nothing to worry about.

To clip the guard hairs under the eye, you can also hold the eyelid partly or completely closed, only this time, you fold the eyelash up, raising it by putting your finger or thumb under it. Fold it and hold it against the lid, while you clip the lower guard hairs.

CLIPPING THE EARS

Because the ears are a sensitive area, most horses will move at least a little while you work on them. If a horse is likely to give you any trouble at all, you had best restrain him right from the beginning, with the mildest restraint you can get by with.

When clipping under the eye, fold the eyelashes up and back and hold them flat.

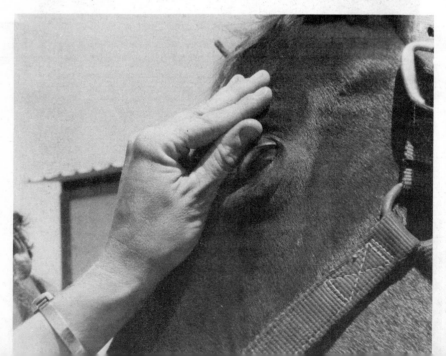

If a horse jerks while the clippers are inside his ear, he can be cut by the blades. Once a horse has been hurt by clippers, he generally gets worse and worse each time you work on him, because he is expecting trouble.

There are two ways to clip ears. The first is to clean the ear and tip completely. The second is to leave a small tuft, or tip of hair, on the end of the ear. A secret longtime used by gaited horse trainers, this adds a pointed effect to the ear. If you look at the photo of the Palomino AQHA stallion Hug N Tuff, each ear was done differently to illustrate this point. His left ear (on your right) was done with a tuft or tip left on. His right ear was shaven clean with no tip left. Trainer Lew Silva, who clipped the ears, likes the tuft left on and felt a view of both

To show the difference in ear clipping, Hug N Tuff's left ear (on your right) was clipped with the pointed tuft left on. His other ear was clipped with a blunt cut at the tip.

types of clipping would show you how that tip can enhance an ear.

Even if you twitch your horse to restrain him for ear clipping, it doesn't mean you should dive right in and begin doing the ear. Before you begin to clip, take your hand and gently rub the ear a little, inside and out. This gives the horse a chance to get an idea of what is about to take place.

When you begin, go down the outside of each edge, coming down very lightly with the size 40 blade. Go to the inside, getting most of the longer hair out, then bend the ear slightly back so you can have better access to the inside. You will find that bending the ear outward helps especially when you are cleaning out the hair in the natural fold in the inside bottom part of the ear.

While you still have the horse restrained, you may wish to take a lightly oiled rag and clean the dirt and scale out of the

Begin by working down, cleaning out the inside hairs.

Fold this section out, to enable you to easily clip in and around the natural fold of the ear.

Work down each edge.

Work up in alternate strokes.

The ear should be flawlessly clipped, as this one has been.

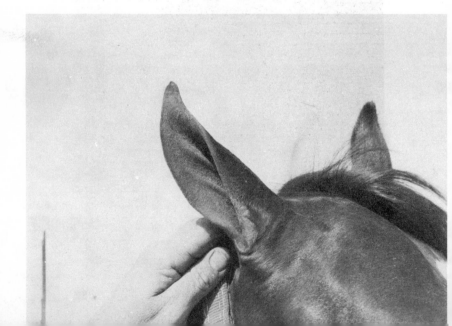

ear after it is clipped. Then remove the twitch, if you have used one, and gently rub the horse on the nose to end on a good note.

CLIPPING THE BRIDLE PATH

How far back should a bridle path go? The length has always been controversial. Some say that a horse with a heavy throatlatch and neck looks better with a longer bridle path. This seems a little strange to me. I would rather hide that type of throatlatch than clean off the hair a long way back on the bridle path and make the thickness even more visible.

Clipping the bridle path.

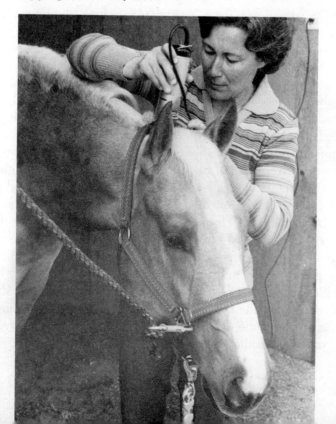

If a horse has a nice head and a small, clean throatlatch, you can bring his bridle path back about ten inches and show off the nice neck. If you have a bad-headed horse, don't come back as far.

Sometimes experimentation works best. Begin by clipping the shortest bridle path you can get by with. Smooth down the mane and stand back and look, from a distance, at the overall picture. If you think you need a longer bridle path, work on it about an inch at a time until it is where you think it looks best. Just remember that you can always make it longer, but once you have one that is too long, it takes a great deal of time to grow the hair out to mane length again in order to shorten the bridle path.

How far forward should it go? There is a bone between the horse's ears that is your guideline on how far forward to clip a bridle path. If you drew a straight line from the back of one ear across to the back of the other, you would be crossing that bone that feels like a nob. Never clip forward of that nob, or you will be taking off too much forelock.

When clipping, you use the size 40 blade, and it is best to clip the bridle path about two days before the show. If you have a good haired horse, you only have to clip the bridle path itself. If the horse has a little too much coat, hairs will be sticking up alongside the freshly cut bridle path, which would necessitate a careful job of blending. When you do have to blend, such as in the case of a horse that is not completely shed out, don't cut too deeply on the side of the bridle path. Blend the hairs by slanting the clipper blades up a little, or turning them over. By clipping too close on the side, you change the coat color: a sorrel horse, when clipped close, goes to dun; a black horse goes to grey; and so on.

If you clip between shows, it is a good idea to clip to about an inch away of the start of the mane. If you go all the way to the mane each time, you will be taking a few extra hairs with you, and your bridle path will get longer and longer.

When you begin to clip, don't start right off cutting against the grain of the hair. Particularly if the horse is not used to being clipped, it is better to start near the mane and work forward, rather than start at the ears and coming down. Go up toward the ears, working up from the mane, once or twice until you feel the horse relax, then you can start at the ears and work down, cutting against the grain. With a touchy horse, it may take longer to get him to accept it.

Before you begin to clip near the ear and work down, put your hand or arm against the ear nearest to you and gently push it forward enough to keep it out of your way, and to settle the horse if he is worried about having his ears touched.

The first section of mane occasionally wants to stick up and will not lay flat as it should. If you take the clippers and cut a small patch at an angle under the mane (on the side on which the mane falls), the mane will lay better.

HANDLING THE LEGS WHILE CLIPPING

The easiest way to clip a horse is to have him stand squarely on all fours and not move a muscle while you are clipping. Some horses haven't read this book, and they would rather move around while you clip! If your horse is touchy and insists on moving, try one of these methods to secure him:

1. While you are clipping one leg, have someone hold up the opposite one. This puts all the horse's weight on the leg you are clipping and he has to remain stationary.

2. If you're by yourself and you are clipping one leg, reach under with the free hand and pinch the tendon of the other leg. This will also encourage the horse to stand firm on the leg you are clipping.

3. Squat down aways and lay the horse's front leg over your knee. Let it hang there in a relaxed manner. Do not try to lock onto it. You can work all the away around the foot like this.

When clipping one leg, it helps to have a helper hold up the opposite leg, so that the horse is forced to anchor the one you are working on.

Hanging a relaxed leg over your knee is a good way to get a smooth clip job.

Don't think you can keep the horse from putting it down, however; if he decides to he will. But this method often will have him momentarily buffaloed into holding still.

4. When working on the hind foot, hang it over your knee the same way you did with the front leg, but remember not to raise it way up like a horseshoer would. The horse doesn't have the same range of motion in back as he does in front, and he will be more comfortable if the foot is held low. As you clip in this manner, when you get around to the back of the pastern and fetlock area, pull the toe of the hoof forward for easier access to the back of the leg.

5. If you are clipping up the sides of the cannon bone and are having trouble getting into the nooks and crannies between the tendons, pick the leg up as you would to clean a hoof. This smoothes out the side of the legs and allows for better clipping.

6. If you are on one side of the horse, such as the left, and you are preparing to clip the inside of the other (right) leg, do work from the side you are on. That is the only way you can clearly see the inside of that leg. You may want to hold up the left leg or pinch the tendon, as you reach under the horse to do the inside of the right leg. This way, you won't have to stick your head around a leg and way under the horse to see what you are clipping.

CLEAN-UP OR TOUCH-UP LEG CLIPPING

If a horse has a fine, short hair coat or was previously booted and needs just a touch-up, you have very little to do. Using a size 10 or 30 blade (a 10 is best), hold the clippers at a sideways angle and feather all the way around the coronary band. When you do the back of the fetlock and pastern area, reverse the clippers, working down the leg. Feather the newly clipped hair with the unclipped so it lays flush. You do not want a definite separation. Everything should look natural. Back behind the pastern, you can work up, as long as you work down just as often to feather.

Holding the clippers at this angle, work around the coronary band.

When clipping the back of the cannon bone, fetlock and pastern area, reverse the clippers and work down.

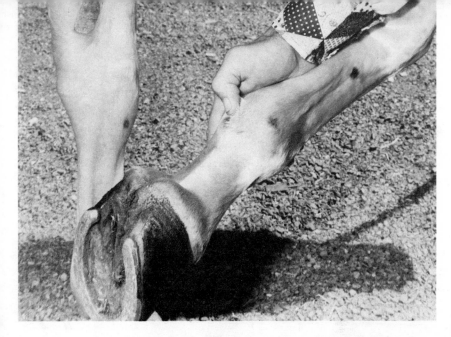

The ergot must be removed in order to get a smooth clip in that area.

Removing Ergots and Chestnuts

An ergot is the small, bony growth on the back of the fetlock. Like the chestnuts, it is a leftover from evolution and serves no purpose. You *must* remove the ergots in order to get a clean, smooth clipping job, and you will still have to work hard at getting all those fine hairs which line the area around the ergots.

It's possible to just hold the ergot between your thumb and forefinger and twist until it comes off. Or, a pair of hoof nippers, a razor blade or a good pair of scissors will take it off. Be sure to trim it flush to the line of the leg, but not dig any deeper. If it is stubborn about coming off, it may have to be saturated with water or oiled before you can get it off.

The chestnuts are above the knee on the inside of the leg. Each time you give your horse a bath, and his legs are wet, use your fingernails or a dull pocket knife and peel off excess chestnut. These, too, should lay flush with the line of the leg. Some

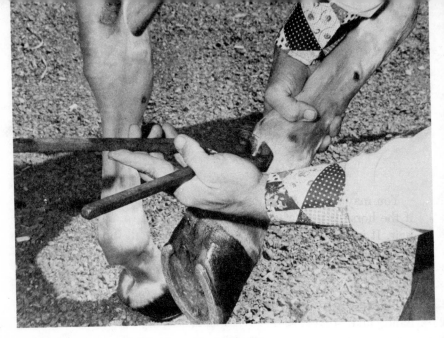

Hoof nippers work well in removing ergots.

Chestnuts must be peeled off so that they are flat against the line of the leg.

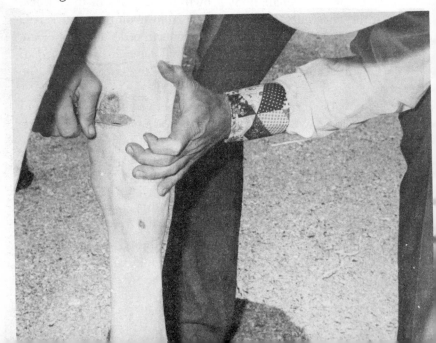

older horses get extremely large, brittle ones. In this case, you may have to nip off the first part with hoof clippers, then carefully pick off the rest. Again, do not go too deeply.

Leg Clipping and Booting

You may need to do more of a clipping job than a touch-up if the horse is not completely shed out, or if he has heavy leg hair. It is very advisable to clip white socks all the way to the top to give a clean look. White hair is generally thicker than dark, and when you clip the white socks, they look more in line with the darker ones.

Before you decide to clip up higher than just the coronary band, take some things into consideration. First, if you clip

White socks, if clipped all around, will appear neater and will be easier to keep white.

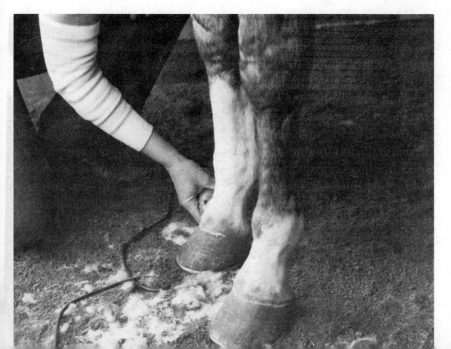

a dark legged horse, you are going to temporarily change his coat color—black to grey, chestnut to dun, etc. If you boot a horse with the clippers and he has dark legs, it is best to do it at least two weeks prior to a show so the natural color returns. Then, you have only to touch up around the coronary band and behind the leg.

Do you have a Paint horse with high stockings above the knees and hocks? I have three of them and I find the only way to keep the leg stain-free and clean looking, and the hair short, is to clip them all the way up above the knees and hocks and taper the hair at the top, working it neatly into the unclipped hair. With white legs, you can actually boot a horse the day before a show, if you use a size 10 blade, blend carefully, and take your time. They will look perfectly smooth.

AVOIDING CLIPPER MARKS ON THE LEGS

Some people have a tendency to race around the legs, working up and down frantically to get the big job done. Take your time. You may wish to do two legs one day, while booting, and the other two the next day. This also keeps your clippers from overworking and heating up. Be sure the hair is *clean* before you clip the legs, and if you should work up the leg and get clipper lines, the best you can do to erase them is to go back and forth, horizontally, across the lines. It shortens some of the longer, vertical lines of hair that are left when the clippers dig and leave marks, and helps erase the problem partially. But the best way to avoid clipper marks in the first place is to clip slowly and carefully and to never use overheated clippers.

BODY CLIPPING . . . GOOD OR BAD?

Most successful halter fitters have very few kind words to say about body clipping. They would much rather shed a horse out naturally and have the rich, deep color and soft coat.

Body clipping definitely changes color and the color stays muted until the horse either grows out a great deal, or sheds later on—usually the following year. When you body clip a palomino, it turns nearly white; and a light bay will turn to a somewhat muley color.

A bad coat cannot be improved by body clipping. It *can* be shortened, but if it was not shiny before clipping, it is not going to be shiny right after. A bad coat only looks worse when it has been clipped.

There are times when clipping must be done and, if it is done correctly, it may serve your immediate purpose. It should not, however, be done as a shortcut, in place of good feeding and grooming, the things that produce a good natural coat. When you body clip a horse, you *must* take good care of him, possibly even more so than the non-body clipped horse, to get the coat in top condition.

You may decide to body clip a horse prior to a show in the fall because he has haired-up more quickly than expected, or you might have just purchased him and the former owners didn't keep his coat short. You will find that weanlings are notorious for having heavy coats and hairing-up fast when fall approaches, and if they are entered in halter futurities, you might need to clip. Just remember that you are always better off working hard for a natural coat.

If you feel you *must* body clip, follow these guidelines:

1. Be sure to thoroughly wash the horse prior to body clipping. A dirty coat will clog up your clippers and cause them to drag and cut irregularly. A clean coat is easy to clip because it stands up.
2. Whenever possible, use large clippers, such as the Sunbeam Clipmaster, for the neck and body areas, and Oster size 10 blades on the small Oster clippers (or the equivalent) for the head, legs, and hard to reach creases. If you do not have large

clippers, the Oster size 10 blade will suffice for the entire horse, but you must let it cool when it overheats.

3. When you come to areas, such as the chest, that have cowlick type hair arrangements, you must clip against the grain of each swirl of hair. Try grabbing the skin with your hand and stretching it flat.

4. Do the legs last, and be extra sure they are clean. When you bathed your horse prior to the clipping, some of the dirt rinsing off the body might have stayed in the legs.

5. Spray your clippers, or dip them in oil, frequently during clipping.

6. After clipping, bathe your horse again to remove any hidden debris or loose hair. Many people bathe then, this time, rinse with warm water with a small amount of olive oil or baby oil added to the rinse water to smooth out the coat.

7. *Never blanket a body clipped horse with one that causes friction to the clipped hair.* Unlined canvas blankets and other types can rub harshly against the hair and give it a singed look. The best blanket and hood to use on a clipped horse is the nylon lined set that will do no "friction burning" of the hair.

8. If you body clip for a specific show or sale, do it at least two weeks before the event so that the hair will grow out some by show or sale time and look more natural.

RESTRAINING

The guideline for using restraints is to use *only as much as absolutely necessary*, and no more. If you can get the job done by using a mild twitch, fine. If you can gently fold an ear down and "hold" the horse, fine. But if your instinct is to "nail the horse to the ground" so he will stand, and you decide to resort to tranquilizer to do the job, it can get you in trouble.

In states such as California, it is illegal to use tranquilizers on any horse competing in a horse show. You may not even consider tranquilizing your horse for this purpose, but you might give your horse a shot to calm him in order to clip his ears, then three or four days later, when you get to the horse show, there still might be enough tranquilizer in his system to show up in a drug test.

Too, you should not *rely* on tranquilizers. The use of a drug might quiet a nervous or restless horse, but it is certainly not going to change his mind about anything—particularly if he hates having his ears clipped. I once borrowed a horse from a friend to show and get ready for a sale. The horse was so bad about his ears that we took him to the vet to have him tranquilized and restrained in the stocks, so we could clip his ears a week prior to the sale, giving plenty of time for the drug to leave his system. After the first shot, the gelding acted "drunk" enough to work on—until the clippers were turned

After threading the lip cord through the loop, as shown, tie it off just below the loop. All you need to do when the horse needs more restraint is tug lightly on the lip cord.

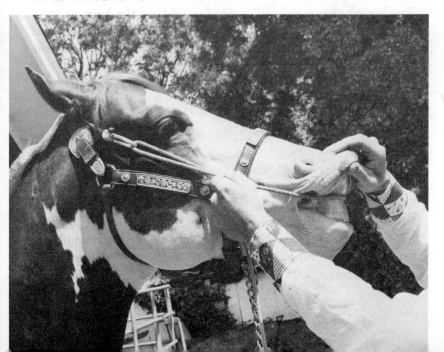

on. He was then just as strong as ever and fought just as much. Another shot, and he seemed even more under, but it still took one person to cover his eyes, a second to ear down one ear, and still another with the clippers to try to clip. The job got done, but I can't help feeling there had to be a better way!

A Look at Physical Restraints

Lip Cord   Basically a restraint, this is a method of training a horse to accept clipping. The nylon cord goes around the head and into the area between the upper lip and gums, and is tied off on the side of the head. When the horse begins moving, you can lift up and gently shake the side of the lip cord to put more pressure on the lip. When the horse is good, relax it.

Twitching   There are two types of twitches commonly used today. The first is the standard chain loop twitch with a long wooden handle. When you use this, never stand in front of the horse. If he were to rear and swing the handle, it could knock you for a loop. When applying the twitch, gently put the upper lip through the chain and twist it slowly, just enough to hold it there. You definitely need an assistant to hold this type of twitch while you do the clipping. When the horse becomes a problem, you can then tell your helper to tighten the twitch. Again, it should only be as much pressure as needed. Minimum pressure, not maximum. Tighten a little when the horse is bad, loosen a little when he is good. And, when you remove the twitch, do remember to rub his nose gently for that happy ending.

The second type of twitch, sometimes known as the humane twitch, is one that will stay on the horse without someone holding it. It is put into place and snapped into the halter ring. It can be adjusted loosely, or a little tighter, as the case may be. The only danger with this type of twitch is that, with an extremely spooky horse that might try to rear or go over backward, a handler can't undo it fast enough to stop a storm. On

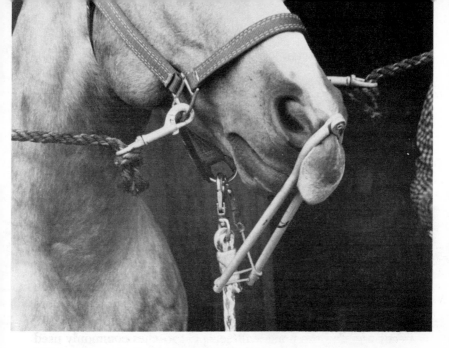

This type of twitch can be used when you have no one to help by holding the standard chain twitch with the wooden handle.

a quiet horse, however, it is often the most effective restraining device to use when you are clipping a horse without help.

EARING DOWN A HORSE

Many people are against holding a horse's ear to restrain him because they feel it makes a horse headshy. If you grab the ear and nearly twist it off, and have a wrestling match over the idea, you will certainly have problems. But, if you ear a horse correctly, it is a good way to apply proper restraint.

Don't be harsh. Never grab an ear suddenly, with your hand coming out of nowhere. Instead, if you plan to hold the left ear, stand on the left side of the horse. Put your left hand gently on his nose, then rub his neck with your right hand and work your way slowly up to the ear. He will accept the feel of the hand on the ear much more readily if you do it this way.

Take hold of the ear and be sure you have it at the base, where it joins the head. Use only as much restraint as necessary and do it by just bringing the ear slightly down. *Do not twist it.* When you are done, rub the ear and the neck gently.

ANOTHER METHOD OF EARING

There seems to be a nerve at the base of the ear, on the side nearest the forelock. If you can gently place your hand around the base of the ear, in the manner stated above, you can push your fingernails into this nerve at the ear base to hold the horse still. This works especially well when you have no help. You can clip it as you hold the ear, because you are not holding it closed. Again, it must be done with only as much force as necessary, and the horse will accept it if you approach it gradually.

SHOULDER HOLD

Quite often, all you need to do to restrain a horse is to take a handful of skin, just in front of the shoulder at the start of the neck, and hold it. This is a sensitive area and the hold works well for some horses. They don't have much of an urge to move once a person has a grip there. If you have a bad horse that is wise to a twitch through former misuse, you may want to have one person shoulder hold the horse while the other puts the twitch on, so that the horse does not try to evade the twitch.

CHOOSE YOUR RESTRAINT WISELY

Before you select a restraint, stop to think about what you want to clip, how much restraint you need, and whether or not you have help available. If you are clipping out the inside of the nostrils, you certainly do not want to use a twitch, because it would close up the nose. An ear restraint would be indicated.

If you choose to use the ear restraint in which you press against the nerve, you *will* be able to clip that ear while you hold it. However, if you do not use this method, you may want to use a twitch, or have a helper hold the other ear as you clip.

Too, you might try just keeping the horse contained. Sometimes, merely backing a horse into a corner tells him he might as well send up the surrender flag, and he will give in to you. Many horses respond better to this than they do total restraint in stocks. It just depends on the horse. Give your horse, and yourself, plenty of time to figure each other out, and your clipping will be successful.

Chapter 10

Manes and Tails

If you think mane and tail care stops at just thinning, pulling and shaping to the correct thickness and length, you're wrong. While you are fitting your halter horse, caring for the mane and tail is another everyday chore to add to the list. The hair must be conditioned and guarded. If growth is needed, it must be encouraged. The hair must be kept clean and stain-free.

MANES

One of the first problems you'll encounter when bringing a horse in from "outside" to begin fitting him is getting the mane to lay flat. If a horse has been out in the sun and the wind, his mane will likely be sticking out in all directions. No doubt it will be too long, too thick, fuzzy and sunburned. In the case of a weanling, the mane will have that baby texture, and would much rather reach for the sky than lay flat.

If the mane is much too long and is sticking up, you may find that it is better to just thin it and encourage it to lay flat and *shorten it later*. If you get it too short right away, it is likely to have more of a tendency to stick up. Leave it a little long and let its own weight pull it over, as you treat it daily. Just getting out of the wind will help the mane a great deal.

Hand pulling.

THINNING THE MANE

There are three ways to thin a mane. The first is done with the fingers only. Take a section of hair in your left hand and pull it down, holding it securely, between your thumb and forefinger. Now, with your right hand, take another grip, just above the other fingers. Hold tight and push your right hand up. This pushes part of the hairs up, leaving others in your left hand. Since less hairs should be in your left hand, pull down and remove those hairs with a jerk. Continue this throughout the mane. If the horse is greatly bothered by it, you may wish to do a little each day, and spend several days thinning.

Another method of thinning is to use a comb. It's done in somewhat the same manner. You hold a small amount of hairs in your left hand, place the comb above them and comb up. Pull out the remaining hairs with your left hand.

Comb pulling.

Pulling with a clipper blade.

You can do the same type of thinning with a clipper blade, detached from the clippers. Hold the hairs in the left hand, place the blade above the left fingers, in the same manner as the comb, move the blades up, and pull down the remaining hairs.

Why have I not given directions for thinning shears? I feel these often shorten the hair, rather than thinning. The main reason for hand, comb or clipper blade pulling is to remove the extra hairs from the *roots*, removing the complete hair shaft, not just cutting it. If thinning shears are used from underneath the mane, as suggested by some people, you shorten those hairs and the mane bunches up when they begin to grow out.

When the mane is thinned, but not yet shortened (while you're letting the weight pull it over), wash the mane and rinse it thoroughly. Be sure not to leave any soap in it or the dry flaking will cause the horse to rub. When the mane is dry and you blanket your horse, put a hood on him. Be sure that your hood is either completely nylon lined, or lined in the mane area. This keeps friction from rubbing the mane. The nylon does a beautiful job of encouraging the mane to lay flat.

After a few days and nights of wearing a hood, the mane should be laying over better, and now you can think about shortening it. You shorten by using the clipper blade in the same manner as you would in thinning. Grip a small clump of hairs with your left thumb and forefinger. Be sure it's a *small* clump. Push up some of the hairs with the clipper blade. Now, rather than pulling down with your left hand, you take the clipper blade and gently shorten the hairs in the left hand by a plucking motion. By going over and over the mane, doing parts of small clumps of hairs, you get a natural look. You should *never cut a mane with scissors or shave it short with electric clippers*. You want a natural feather, not a chopped look.

When the mane is shortened and thinned, and you're using a hood to encourage it to lay down, remember to wash the mane well, scrubbing well at the roots, at least once a week.

Shortening the mane with a clipper blade.

Brushing the mane with a damp brush encourages it to lay flat.

Also, wash your hood when you see grime building in the nylon by the top of the mane area. Cleanliness will help avoid mane rubbing.

Each day, if the weather permits, remove the hood for a few hours. Go into the stall several times and brush the mane over with a damp brush.

Each day, when you work the horse, rub baby oil into his mane. Start with a light coating, going to heavy, depending on how stubborn the mane is about laying over. Comb the mane down flat and apply a sweat wrap. Work the horse as you would when sweating the neck, leaving the wrap on at least a half hour after the work. When you rinse the neck after removing the wrap, comb the mane flat.

WHEN THE MANE WON'T LAY OVER

There are ways of convincing a mane to lay flat when it is being extremely stubborn. These ways also work well if you do not have a hood to use, or if it's summer and too hot to use a hood.

Braiding   Normal braiding, with small braids pulled down to lay flat, will work with some manes. Wet the hair before braiding. Be careful not to braid so tight that the horse is irritated and tries to rub his mane out. Rebraid every two or three days, washing the mane when necessary.

Braiding and Weighting   After braiding a mane, you may wish to sew in a small, fishing sinker at the end of each braid. This will weight the mane and pull it down.

Banding   Section the hair off in no more than half inch sections. Band it just a short way from the base, and pull the hairs from underneath straight down. You need to pull just a few of those hairs, and the section will lay flat.

MANE LENGTH

A mane about four inches long is very attractive, *if* it is of the texture to lay flat. If you feel it would look better on your horse as an individual, a six-inch mane is also appropriate. When a mane is short, well thinned and properly cared for, it looks extremely nice if you brush it every day with a wet brush, brushing from the area by the bridle path down toward the withers. This encourages the mane to lay down and back, rather than straight down, to add a more streamlined look to the neck.

Daily Conditioning

When you work your horse, keep his mane out of the sun and wind. As mentioned previously, applying baby oil to the mane and covering it with a neck wrap will condition it and help it lay over. It also keeps the sun and wind from damaging the hair while the horse works. Either use this type of "cover," or use a light sheeting hood to protect the mane whenever possible. There are also lightweight mesh neck wraps, called mane tamers, available which can be used during workouts.

The Foretop

The forelock, or foretop, should also be treated with baby oil whenever possible. To show off a horse's head, it is very important that the foretop be of a texture that is not bushy and fuzzy. Baby oil will help keep it smooth. Be sure that you thin the foretop as needed, in the same way as the mane, and shorten it to about eye length or a little shorter.

The Bridle Path

Read the clipping chapter for detail on the bridle path. Remember these guidelines. Don't clip the bridle path all the way back to the mane in between shows. Until you are seriously "show clipping," clip only to within an inch of the mane and leave a small batch of hair sticking up. By clipping all the way down when it is not needed, you will tend to remove a few

Using a neck sweat, after the mane has been saturated with baby oil, will condition it and help it to lay flat.

In banding the mane to lay it over, band in small sections, then pull a few underneath hairs straight down and the sections will lay flat.

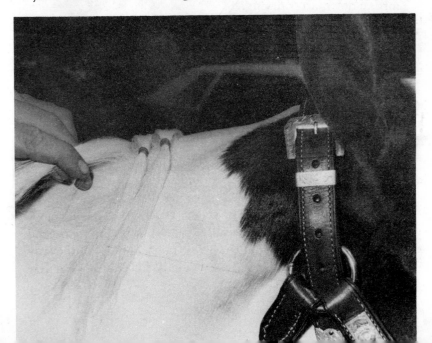

more hairs each time—and soon the bridle path will be far too long.

Don't clip toward the foretop any further than the nob-type bone between the ears. This is located on top of the head, in a straight line from the back of the base of one ear to the base of the other. You can easily feel it.

ADD SOME GLISTEN

Before a show, when you bathe the horse, you may wish to add something to the mane and forelock that gives it an added shine. Hair rinses, available at drug stores, often highlight the hair. Roux Fanciful comes in many colors to treat a white, black or sorrel mane. For the white, use a color such as "White Minx" or some other platinum tone. When the mane is wet, squirt some of the rinse from the bottle, rub it in well, and comb it through the mane. The liquid is generally a purple shade when wet (on the colors used for white hair) and dries with a silver glisten. It also adds some condition and helps the newly washed hair lay down after drying.

THE RUBBED OUT MANE

To revive a rubbed out mane, be sure there is no evidence of scale or irritation at the roots. Clean the neck area and mane well, and brush it daily with *cold water*. This stimulates growth.

THE TAIL

The controversy on tail length and thickness will be alive as long as halter horses are also being used for other things. In California, and other western states, the rage is for long, full tails on Western Pleasure horses. A person who is also haltering one of these horses would probably not want to sacrifice the length of the tail for the sake of the halter class.

Many West Coast horses wear full, long tails, because they are rail horses as well as being shown at halter.

When a horse is being haltered only, it stands to reason that a well thinned tail which has been shortened to just below the hocks will not hinder the judge's view of the good hindquarters, gaskin and cannon bone. A long, full tail can also give the same view to the judge if the top of the tail is properly thinned, and the handler combs through the tail with oil and wraps it tightly with Vetrap about a half hour before a class. Then, when the wrap is slid down and off, the tail is flattened and condensed for the halter class. Before the Western Pleasure class, the tail is shaken out and brushed to the original fullness.

Long or short, a tail needs daily care and it starts with proper shaping. The top of the tail should always be shaped so that it lays flat and doesn't bush out. This is done by hand pulling the hairs from under the sides of the top of the tail. Simply grab a few in your fingers and jerk down to pull them out. When the tail is the proper shape on top, it should be brushed on

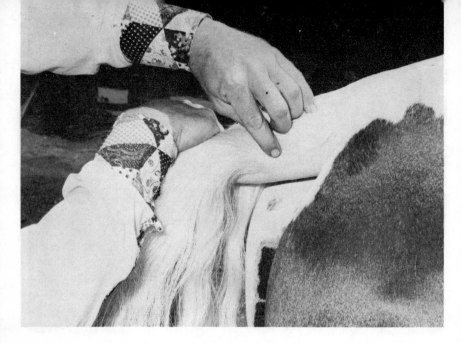

Pulling the underneath and some of the side hairs at the base of the tail bone will help the top hairs lay flat.

top each day with a damp brush. This will encourage stray hairs to hug the dock of the tail and lay flat. Nothing looks worse than a bushy tail top, so work hard to keep it laying flat.

To Comb or Not to Comb

I never touch a tail with a metal comb. I feel something made of plastic or hard rubber is much less harsh to the hairs. If you split too many hairs, the tail will become bushy. So, should you comb through a tail every day?

If you rub baby oil through a tail, so a brush or comb will gently slide rather than harshly pull, you *can* work through the tail each day, but it's not necessary. The only real exception to combing at all is with the tail that rolls up into countless little spirals. This type of tail takes a great deal of work. Each spiral must be unwound by hand, gently pulling the hairs to

Pull hairs out, a few at a time, to thin the tail.

separate them. Only after all are unwound can you comb through the tail, and it should be well oiled.

Pulling Thin

If you decide to pull the tail thinner, reach up inside and pull a few hairs at a time. Simply pull them straight out. Work from several different areas, so you get an even distribution of pulling. You can also just run a gloved hand down through the tail, pulling out hairs as they need to come out. If a tail is horribly thick, you can pull it thinner in the same way as you would a mane, using the clipper blades. Be sure to flatten the tail often, gently brushing it, during this process to check and see if it's the correct thickness. Just pulling and pulling, without checking, might end in a tail that is too thin.

If you wish to shorten the tail, for instance, to have it fall just below the hocks, you can shorten the hairs, by pulling them

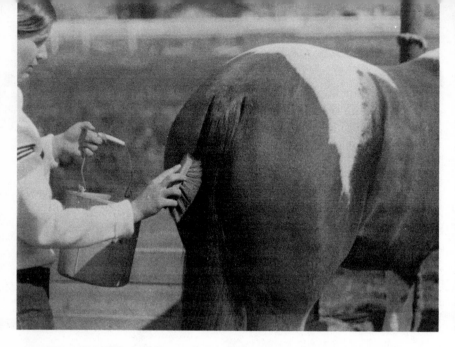

Dampen and brush the top hairs daily to keep them flat.

Running your hands down the tail daily will keep stray hairs flat, rather than bushing out.

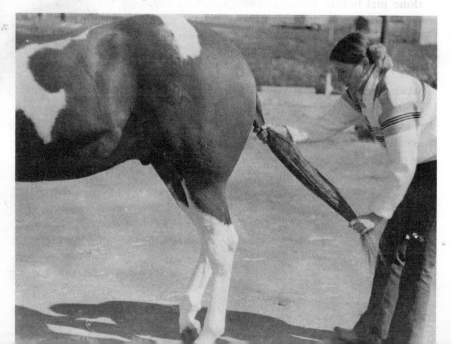

off with your fingers, or with the clipper blade. Always do just a few at one time, and try to shape it so that the underneath hairs taper, shortening from the gaskin area, feathering down. You don't want a "blunt cut" look.

PROTECTION FROM SUN AND WIND

During daily work, the tail can be damaged by sun and wind as much as the mane if not more, because of the way it flies out and "trails behind." To condition and protect the tail, treat it with baby oil and wrap it every day as you work your horse. You would wrap the tail the same way as you would for shipping.

WRAPPING THE TAIL

When you wrap a tail for shipping or working, you do it by flipping hairs up inside the wrap, to keep it from slipping off. Remember never to leave wraps on for long periods of time or you may cut off the circulation. Especially with a tight wrap done just before a class, you may cause harm by leaving it in too long.

Let's assume you're using track bandages for wrapping during hauling, or everyday work. Start at the *middle* of the tail and take one wrap. Flip a little hair up into the bandage and wrap over it. Wrap to the top of the tail, consistently clipping a few hairs into each rotation around the tail. Now, wrap down, all the way to the bottom of the tail. If it's a long tail, you may wish to fold up the end, and wrap it so that no hair at all is exposed. Especially when you have a white tail, this is a good way to protect it from stains.

When you finish wrapping and flipping hairs, you may wish to put a second track bandage over the first, to cover the flipped hairs. When you remove these wraps, the tail will be sticking up in places where hair was flipped. Brushing with a damp brush will straighten it out.

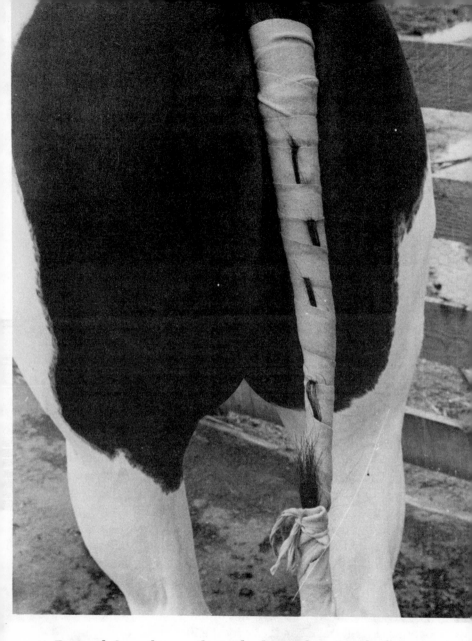

During daily work, wrap the tail by flipping hairs into the first wrap (left). Then, cover it with a second track bandage (right).

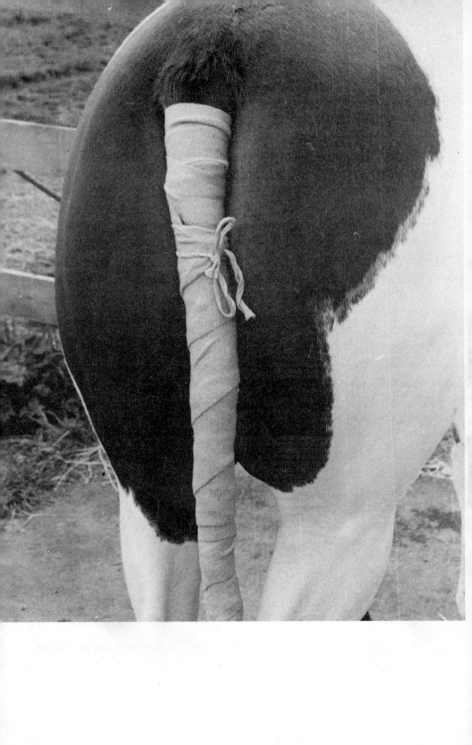

Wrapping Before a Class

If you've wrapped your horse to haul, and removed the wraps at the show to straighten out the flipped hairs, you will want to rewrap until your class. A half hour to an hour before your class, treat the tail with baby oil or a standard coat spray and conditioner and work it through gently with a plastic or rubber comb. Smooth it with your hands. Wrap it with track bandage or Vetrap, being careful to keep the top of the tail smooth. *Do not* flip hairs now, because you want the tail smooth by class time. Just before your class, pull down to remove the wrap and use your hands to do any smoothing necessary on the tail.

To Help the Tail Grow

Some horses need to grow more tail, rather than have it taken away. In this case, go into the stall once or twice a day and use a regular body brush (stiff) to encourage growth. Dip the brush in *very cold* water and brush with the lay of the hair at the top, being sure to get clear to the skin with the water. Remember that the tail grows from the roots at the dock, so saturate them with the cold water.

Chapter 11

Dressing the Halter Horse

Show halters are a big expense. They must be properly chosen, fitted to the horse to show his head to the best advantage. And, you must care for your halter as the investment it is.

What are the characteristics of a good show halter? Silver halters are naturally needed for important shows. If you're a youngster showing in small shows, you probably can't invest in a silver halter. Whether you can or can't go that far, the *fit* and *style* of the halter enters into the picture first.

A good halter conforms to the head and highlights it. The headpiece must be short enough so that there is not a great deal of excess "trailing" down the side of the halter. If you use the same halter on two horses, you might consider having two sets of headpieces, which is easily done if you have the type of halter which buckles on both sides of the headpiece. All you need to do, when switching your halter from your yearling to your two-year-old, for example, is to change to the larger, longer headpiece and adjust the halter under the jaw. Any good saddle maker, who makes halters and headstalls, can make you an extra headpiece.

The sidepiece of the halter, which goes from the area in line of the throatlatch down to the ring in which the noseband connects, shouldn't be excessively long. About 8½ inches is the maximum length. If it is too long, it makes the head of the horse appear longer. A shorter sidepiece "closes up" the head.

American Paint Horse Association stallion, Rooster Cogburn.

The halter on this weanling filly was borrowed from her yearling big sister. If the halter had a smaller extra headpiece, this halter could be adjusted to fit this filly without the extra headpiece leather trailing down the side of her face.

And, when you change your halter from your two-year-old back down to your yearling by altering the headpiece, the sidepiece will not look too long for that horse. If the sidepiece is too long, the throatlatch section of the halter will set too high and not fit as neatly as it should.

Many of the high quality, newer show halters have wires in the throatlatch, hidden in the rolled leather. This allows you to shape it perfectly around the jaw, so that when you change the halter from horse to horse, it can be "customized" to fit his head.

The gullet of the halter is the piece which goes down the center under the jaw, from the throatlatch to the curb strap. Because you want everything to fit flat against the horse's head, this gullet must be of a type that has no protruding buckles or loose, flopping, excess leather. If the halter has a wire base throatlatch, it eliminates the need for a buckled gullet, for you can take up, or let down, the halter by moving the throatlatch wire. If you do not have a wire throatlatch, choose a halter with an adjustable gullet, but one without a great deal of bulk. You want to show off the jaw line with a nearly "invisible" gullet.

The curb straps of the halter should be adjustable. Again, you want a smooth, tight fit. If you try to take a big halter way in to fit a very small horse, you'll have extra leather flopping under the jaw–chin area. Be sure to pick a halter with a gullet that fits your needs, so that it is at its maximum "letout" stage for your larger horse, and needs only be taken up a small amount for your smaller horse.

Any adjustable straps on your halter should have keepers, so that no protruding "leftovers" can be seen. The halter must

Casper Amigo is wearing a properly fitted halter for her small head size.

neff

fit like the horse was "poured" into it, close to the head with nothing detracting from the smooth appearance.

Adjusting the Halter on Your Horse

We've already established that the halter should fit snugly on the head. If you have a headpiece which buckles on both sides, take it up equally on each of the sides to keep the tension the same on each side of the halter.

The headpiece should not be too far behind the ears. Always slide it up close to the base of the ear. This adds to the correct, smooth, tight look. If you have silver keepers at the ends of the headpiece, don't tuck them into the ring at the side of the halter.

The ring which joins the noseband and curb strap with the sidepiece should fit right up under the bone of the jowl. If it's much under that point, tighten your halter to bring it up. It must fit snug and high, or it will detract from your horse's head, making it look longer.

Keep the throatlatch down in the natural crease of the top of the jowl on the sides, fitting high and close under the throatlatch area itself. It should always "hug" the horse, and not protrude. If it's a little long, pull it down under the jaw, so that the tiny bit of excess is hidden.

Keep the curbstrap snug with any leather ends tucked into their respective keepers. The curbstrap, as well as the gullet, should lay flat. If you have a bend in the gullet, out away from the horse, it's too long.

Matching the Halter to the Head

The rule of thumb in choosing a halter is that if your horse has a small, pretty head, you flaunt it. If the head is larger and not as attractive, you hide it. Let's say you have a weanling or yearling filly. She has an exquisite head. Your choice of

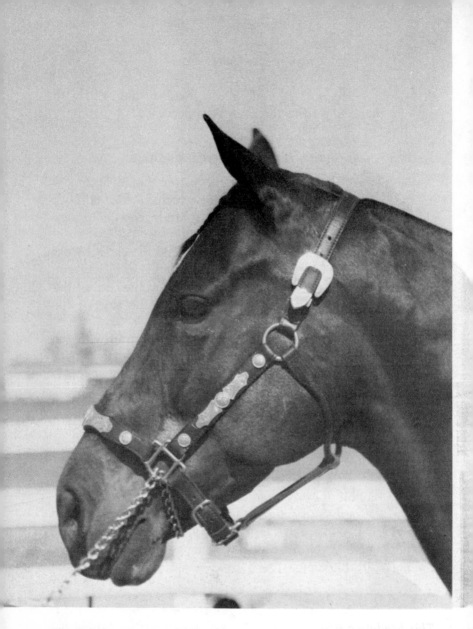

This halter is improperly fitted. It does not hug the head.

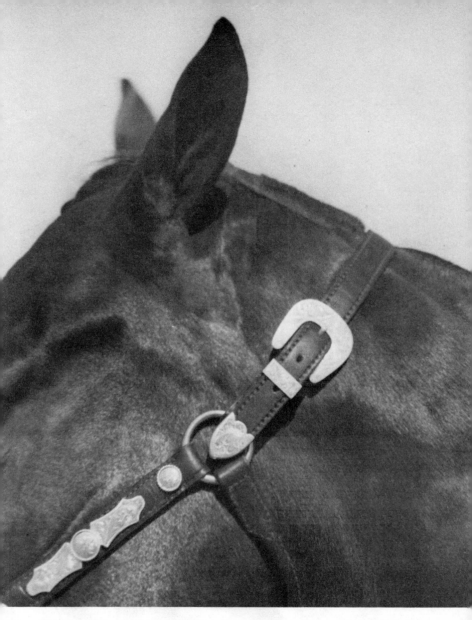

This headpiece is improperly adjusted. It rests too far behind the ears.

Same head, same halter, but now it is properly fitted to the horse. The adjustment has been made to bring it up higher near the jowl, so the noseband and curb straps don't hang too low. The headpiece has been pushed up to just behind the base of the ear.

halter would be one of a narrow width. Rather than filling the leather with wide silver bars, you would choose delicate scrolls or dainty filigree.

If you have a filly that is not as feminine, and her head is not as small, you can use a wider leather width and more "powerful" silver. There's more room on a larger head, so you fill up the "extra space."

Stallions are masculine, so you can definitely dress them with wider, more ornate halters, but don't make them so large and gaudy that you cover a *good head* on a halter stallion. You

The three points to adjust:
1. *Push the headpiece up to the base of the ears.*
2. *The side ring should be adjusted so that its top rests in the groove just below the bone of the jowl.*
3. *The throatlatch lays flat in the groove of the jowl and throatlatch area, and is connected to a gullet which lays flat against the underside of the jaw.*

follow the same rule of thumb—flaunting the nice head and covering up the bad one—but a stallion's halter should not be "feminine." A thin, filigreed, dainty halter would look out of place on a 1250 pound stallion.

Halters have gotten away from the straight leather look, and many of them have scalloped leather, contoured to specific patterns of shaped silver bars, or concho-type silver mountings. These look nice on mares, stallions and geldings, depending on the width of the scalloping and the amount of silver, and how it fits your needs.

Dress your gelding as a gelding, and not as a mare. Keep away from the dainty feminine halters, but follow that same rule of thumb. If he's a big, stout gelding, with a not-so-tiny head, he can wear a wider halter with more silver. If he has an attractive head, thin things down.

The Lead Shank

The hardware in your lead shank should match that in your halter. Silver on the shank is optional, and you may find there is no real need for it. When purchasing a shank, be sure that the snap at the end of the chain fits through the ring fittings on your halter. Then, decide how you'll rig your shank when you show your horse.

Loop Only, Through Bottom Ring   This gives you the least amount of control. Many horses don't need much restraint or correction, and this type of arrangement will work.

Loop With Knot   By tying a knot in the shank, as shown in the photograph, the chain remains twisted and stays together, not flopping apart. This knot also acts as a safety measure. If the snap should work loose, the knot will hold the chain in place.

Chain Under the Chin   When the chain is rigged under the chin, it goes through the offside (right side) ring and up to the top side ring of the halter. This method of rigging the chain

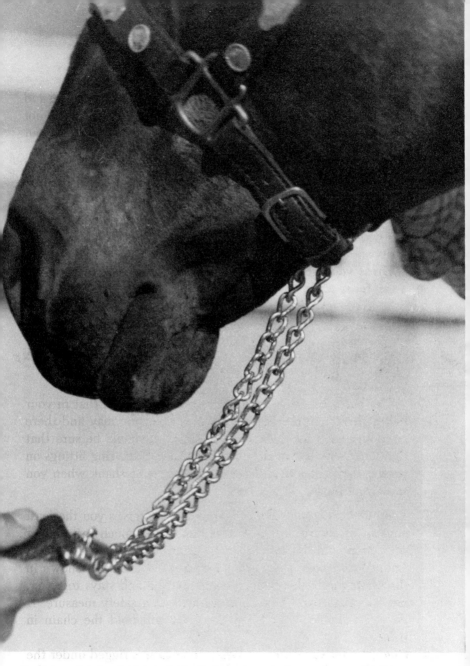

Looping the shank through the halter ring, and snapping it back at the lead portion allows minimum control.

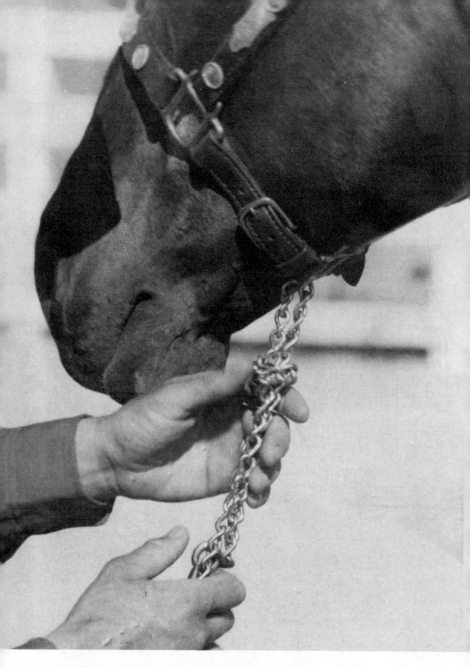

Looping the shank, with a knot tied in for safety.

Chain under chin.

Chain over nose.

Chain through mouth.

gives you control without much chance of hurting the horse. Remember that whenever you shank a horse, you instantly release. Never hang onto the chain for more than an instant.

Chain Over the Nose   We're progressively getting more control, as well as severity. The chain over the nose places the shank in a sensitive area. You can't shank a horse as hard this way as when the chain is under the chin or you risk injury to the nose, and you may possibly cause a permanent bump to appear. When you're "guarding with your life" the appearance of your halter horse's nice head, you surely don't want to damage it. If you use the shank chain over the nose, be careful.

Chain Through the Mouth   Many people use this, the most severe method of control, for stallions which are known to be hard to handle in the ring. Remember that the tongue and mouth are sensitive areas, and you must use only as much pressure as you absolutely need.

When you're using that shank, no matter how it is rigged on the halter, *keep all the slack out!* The chain should fit snugly against the horse. You don't want the nice fitting look of a snug halter flawed by loose chain dangling under the chin, down over the nose, or hanging underneath the jaw in a large loop.

CLEANING YOUR HALTER

If you have one of the newer show halters, the silver is mounted on with Chicago screws. This allows you to remove all the silver and polish it while it's off the halter. If you do not have this type of silver mounting, and the silver is on permanently, your cleaning technique will be different.

Clean the leather first, if the silver is a permanent mount. By using a preparation such as Leather New, or Lexol, you can clean the leather and more or less coat it so that the silver polish doesn't penetrate the leather.

There are many ways to clean silver. Some preparations, such as Haggerty's Silversmith Spray Polish, retard tarnish for several months, which leaves you very little to do between shows outside of just wiping the silver and buffing a little with clean cloths.

Silversmith polishing rags allow you to remove the tarnish from unsprayed and untreated silver. The tarnish is loosened by rubbing with the rag, then rubbed off with a clean polishing rag.

Pastes as well as liquids can be used on silver, but be careful not to spread them onto the leather. If you choose one of these types of cleaners, you may try applying it with a *very* soft brush, such as a toothbrush. If the type of cleaner you use must be rinsed off with water, you're at a definite disadvantage, for you must keep the leather dry.

When you use rags for polishing silver, and for last minute touch-ups before a class, be sure the rag is clean. *Never* use the same rag for the silver as you used for the leather, or you'll be transferring oily film onto your sterling.

Al Anderson shows Top Don to a win at Cow Palace. He uses the looped shank with knot.

Al Anderson winning Cow Palace with Bright Coke Plaudit. The lead shank is rigged under the chin on this stallion.

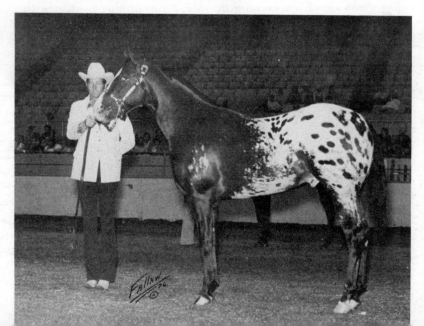

SILVER ... YES OR NO

An expensive silver halter is often out of the question for exhibitors. If you cannot afford one, choose an attractive leather halter that fits well as previously described. Top halter horse fitter, Stretch Bradley, once won a class at the World Championship Quarter Horse show and also at the Congress with a plain leather halter with only a silver buckle, keeper and tip. The halter was so nicely fit to the horse that one of its type could be used even without the little amount of silver it had. The most important element with a halter, silver or not, is fit—and neatness also counts.

Chapter 12

Showing the Halter Horse

Today's halter classes are tough. They require a well trained horse that can enter the ring and set up the instant he's asked. He has to be responsive and attentive. And this well trained halter horse must be so well groomed and perfectly turned out for the class that no flaws can be found.

Let's assume that you are showing in a situation where you have to stall your horse at the showgrounds. If you arrive the day before the show, and you bathed and clipped your horse at home, you're all set. However, you may need to bathe or rebathe your horse before the classes. So what do you do?

Most showgrounds with stalls have washing facilities, but just in case they are crowded, bring your own hose and sprayer. Many owners of horses with a great deal of white will wash the horses a few hours before the classes, often in the dead of night. This is common at shows where there are multiple judges and the classes are repeated over two days.

PREPARING YOUR HORSE

Bathe your horse well in advance of the class. If it is cool out, put a sheet on him and walk him dry. You may need to rewash the legs after walking him. Take the horse to his stall and tie him. Since you may be bathing in the early morning hours, the horse will need to be fed. If you have a rope net-type hay

Top Texas trainer, Kenny Campbell, shows a young Paint horse.

feeder, you can hang it in the stall and let the horse eat while tied. Not only will this allow him to eat, but it will keep him content so he doesn't paw and raise a dust storm, getting himself dirty as he dries.

If your horse has white legs, you may want to wrap them until just before the class. If so, allow them to dry first, for wrapping a wet leg causes the hair to bunch up and lines from the wrapping are liable to show.

When the horse is dry, brush him, then recover him with a sheet or blanket. Again, at least an hour before the class, give him a thorough grooming, using some coat spray, and then recover him.

To encourage the mane to lay flat, put a light application of a pomade hair dressing on the mane and foretop. This can be purchased at any drugstore or place where human hair preparations are sold. Apply it to the mane, comb it down and put a thin mane tamer on the horse to hold the mane in place until the class.

About a half hour before the class, rub some baby oil into the tail, comb through it gently, smooth it down with your hands and wrap it with a track bandage or Vetrap.

Oil must be applied, with your hands or a rag, to the inside of the ears, the muzzle, inside nostrils, around the mouth, over and around the eyes, and part way up the sides of the face, from the nostrils to the beginning of the bone of the jowl. This highlights the face, especially on a fine coated, dark horse.

If your horse has dark legs, such as a black legged bay, or a dark chestnut, use a corresponding color of shoe polish and paint over the chestnuts on the insides of the legs. If the horse has any scars, paint those also. This will blend them with the hair and give a smoother look.

Hoof black is generally applied to all types of Western halter horses, with the exception of the Appaloosa. A clear dressing is applied to the hooves of the Appaloosa horse to make the striped hooves show off this trait, which is a characteristic of

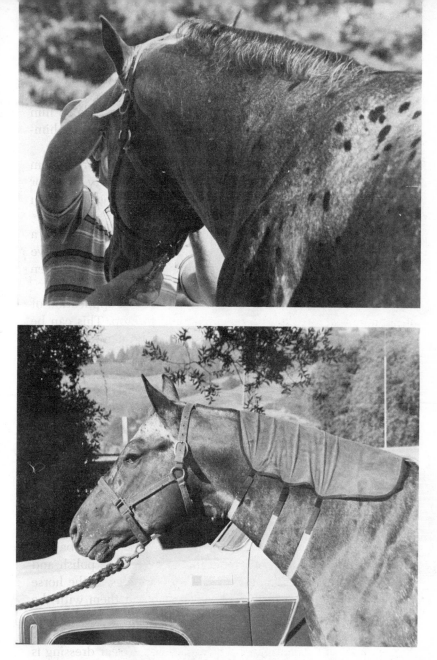

To encourage the mane to lay flat, use a light application of pomade hair dressing and apply a mane tamer until your class.

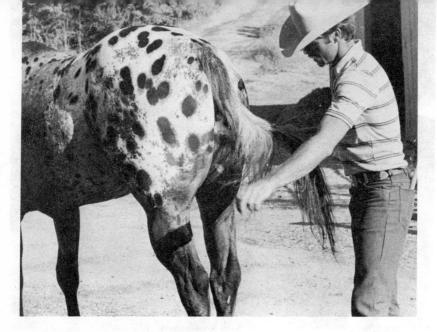

Work baby oil into the tail to produce a glisten.

Used in a California Livestock Symposium demonstration, this horse's face was well oiled and the speaker commented on how this highlights the halter horse.

Apply shoe polish matching the color of the hair to cover scars. It can also be used to cover chestnuts on the legs of dark horses.

the breed. Bring a piece of rubber matting with you and have the horse stand on it while you apply the clear or black hoof dressing. Be sure to make an even line just under the coronary band. Go all the way around the back of the hoof, and when using black, be sure to do the heel and the area just under, so that the hoof looks black from all the way around.

When you're ready to leave for ringside, take a bucket with you to hold your coat spray, fly spray, oil and hoof black for touch-up, and brushes and rags. It's best to lead the horse to the ring either with the sheet on, or to stand him in the shade while waiting for the class to begin. You can touch him up there.

The exception to this rule comes in hot weather, when the horse is brought out and his hair coat stands straight up, adjusting to the heat. In this case, keep the horse moving, with or without the sheet, as you wait for the class, for the increase in body heat will cause the hair to lay back down.

Clean the hoof before applying polish or hoof black.

This Appaloosa was done with clear hoof polish. Other breeds generally use hoof black.

Minutes before the class, put on the show halter, remove the mane tamer and tail wrap and, if the horse has a sheet on, remove it by sliding it off backward toward the tail (not against the hair). Quickly spray the horse lightly with coat spray and wipe him with a cloth or soft brush. Dust off any areas that need it, especially if dust has collected on the oiled face. Now is the time to apply a light coat of fly spray to the legs, under the belly and the barrel. Doing this too soon will cause dust to cling to the horse's legs.

If your horse's white legs were wrapped, remove the wraps, and rub the legs down quickly to smooth the hair.

Your horse's show halter should now be rigged with the proper type of lead shank, depending on how much control is needed.

Spray the coat lightly with a coat spray.

LEARN THE CLASS ROUTINE

If you're lucky, you weren't in the first class, and you can watch the routine and learn how the class will be judged before you go in. Let's first look at entering the ring.

When I'm in the waiting area, I always keep an eye on the other horses going in the class. If the horses are not being called in by number and I'm free to go in as I wish, I try to pick where I want to be.

If I'm showing a young horse that is inexperienced and might get nervous, I try to find an "old pro" to follow in, so I'll be next to this quiet horse in the line-up. A lot of yearlings have been shown so much they are perfect in the class, so I would want my yearling next to a colt like this.

If I have a colt or filly that is a little small, I try not to enter the ring so that I'll be lined up between two very large horses. It's nice to search for one smaller than yours, and line up next to it.

Let's say you're showing a perfectly groomed, perfectly turned out halter horse. The judge is naturally going to notice it, but it will be noticed even more so if you find one that *isn't* well groomed or turned out, and you line up next to that one!

Some people like to be the first in the ring so that the horses they show are seen first by the judge. This might work for some, but if you have a large class, it might be better to go in last, so your horse is the last one he looked at before he began tallying his sheet.

WALKING IN INDIVIDUALLY

The current trend for halter classes takes away any chance an exhibitor has to "get away with murder." It reveals how well the horse is trained—if he can be stood up square without a person twisting out his hocks, or hand placing a crooked front foot to make it look correct. With this new class routine, each horse enters individually and is led up to the judge and squared

When horses are walked in and set up individually, you have just moments to set your horse up.

right in front of him. It all happens fast, and you have but a few seconds to get the job done—so your horse *must* be well trained.

Stay about at your horse's throatlatch area as you walk straight toward the judge. Look forward, positively, right at the judge. Psych him out. Don't look back at your horse or he'll move crooked, possibly even stop.

Stop your horse right in front of the judge and immediately square him up. This is where you begin to worry about not getting between the judge and your horse, because you don't want to block his view. If the judge is on the right side of your horse, you stand on the left. As he moves, you also move, so that you literally swap sides. You never want to block his view of your horse.

Stand back a little ways from your horse. If you have a very small amount of grain in your hand, which he can smell, the horse will stretch his neck out toward it. This shows off the neck and throatlatch, and will probably get the horse to "give you his ears," aiming them forward as they should be. Don't overdo this, however, or you'll create a nippy horse.

Another reason for standing back a ways is that a horse has monocular vision. If you're right up against the front of his face, he can't see you well. If you stand back, he can, and you'll be able to get his attention, and his ears, more easily.

As you move from side to side in front of your horse, corresponding your moves with that of the judge, know where that person is every moment. When the judge gives you the nod and tells you to trot out, do it instantly! Generally, with this type of ring procedure, you'll be trotting in the same line you walked up on, just extending it. No turns are necessary.

When you trot a horse, don't just jog him slowly out. Show some life. Especially with a stallion, you should trot very quickly

Position yourself at your horse's throatlatch as you walk.

and show his good way of traveling and animation. Keep going until you sense that the judge has had a good look. You can't look back, or your horse is liable to slow down or jog. If you alertly watched the classes before yours, you should have some idea of how far others were trotting down the ring, and how long the judge was actually watching. You can judge your own distance by this.

After trotting, line up parallel with the other horses—or head to tail, depending on the instructions of the class. If you head and tail, be especially careful to keep distance between horses. When you're standing with a horse directly in front of you, you can easily be kicked. When a horse is behind, your horse can take a pot-shot at that one. By all means, if you *do* have a horse that is prone to occasional bad acting, warn the person behind you.

If the horses are lined in parallel, side to side, keep enough distance so that the judge can come to the line and walk completely around your horse, far enough back to get an overall view. You must also space yourself well in case another horse begins giving a handler trouble. If you're close, and the horse next to you moves around, he may bump your horse.

When the judge comes back to the line, be sure to move from side to side, as necessary, to stay out of his way. Remember, don't block his line of vision. Also, don't make any big moves, just "float" quietly from side to side. The judge is supposed to be watching your horse, not you.

WALKING TO THE JUDGE, TURNING, AND TROTTING BACK

When this class routine is used, all the horses generally enter the ring in a line, walk once around, then line up. Horses are pulled out of the line-up one at a time, walked directly to the judge, stood up, turned and trotted away. The chapter on training explained how to school your horse so you walk and trot in the *same tracks*. You have to keep moving on that straight

Lining up parallel.

Head and tail line.

Each horse is pulled out of the line-up individually for judging.

line in order for the judge to get a clear look at the way your horse travels. When you make your turn, it should be done tightly so that you don't make a circle.

HANDLING TROUBLE IN THE RING

When you have a shank on your horse, you can get into trouble if you don't use it properly. If your horse acts up and you need to correct him, give him a quick jerk on the shank, then release *immediately*. If you don't release and instead hang onto his head, you can flip him over backwards, for he'll rear to get away from the pressure.

Some horses fool around and play when you begin to trot them out in front of the judge. If you let the horse do this, the judge can't see him travel correctly. You need to catch him up on this immediately. Give him a sharp jerk on the shank to stop him and back him a few steps, then trot him back out again and make him do it the right way.

Showing stallions is often a problem because they may get studdy in the ring and drop down. You must watch for this, and use your shank or pop the horse on the shoulder or barrel with the end of the leather lead to get his attention. If he's just dropping down (as a gelding will do also) because he's terribly relaxed and nonchalant, wiggle your shank and wake him up. If the class is large and the judge is nowhere near you at the time, you may want to lead the horse in a small circle behind the line and bring him back and stand him up again.

If a class is extremely long, such as the big weanling futurities, there is no reason to ask your horse to stand at attention through the entire class. At one weanling futurity at the Cow Palace, it once took over an hour and a half to judge more than

In large classes, such as this weanling futurity at Cow Palace, allow your horse to relax when the chance arises.

one hundred fillies. In a class like this, there is no way you can hold the attention of any horse, especially a baby, for that long. If you try, you'll get into trouble. Let the horse relax a little, even move him around some, without being too conspicuous. Watch the judge at all times and when you know he's coming your way, stand your horse up. This way, when you want attention and animation from your horse, you'll have it. It won't be gone from overuse.

YOUTH SHOWMANSHIP AT HALTER CLASSES

Youth classes are tough. They're filled with good horses, and with snappily dressed handlers. You have to be on your toes to win a showmanship class. Attention to detail is important here and one of the best assets you can have is a well trained, responsive horse. Then, show him well.

Let's say the judge is asking all contestants to lead in and walk around the ring before lining up. Enter at a brisk walk, positioning yourself near the horse's throatlatch. Your right hand is on the leather, just below the chain part of your shank. The remaining leather is coiled in your left hand. Your hand wraps around it, not through it.

Avoid sticking your elbows way out to the side. Keep your hands up, and your right wrist cocked slightly out. Your eyes should be up. You have to be looking up and ahead, with your chin up, watching where you're going and where the judge is, *never* looking at the ground.

As you walk in, space yourself the same way you would if riding in a Western Pleasure class. Stay at least one horse length behind the horse in front of you. Your horse should have been schooled enough so that you can rate his walk to slow him down or move him out, in order to keep proper spacing. The judge is usually somewhere toward the center of the arena. As you briskly walk in, about every four or five steps turn your head and *look* at the judge. Your head should turn to look, then go back into forward position. Don't just glance out of the corner of your eye.

The class routine will basically be the same as the ones mentioned previously. However, showmanship judges often throw in little things to see if the exhibitors are awake. Always listen to the briefing before the class, then listen closely to what the judge tells you individually. Don't just do what the rest of the class is doing. The judge may have one horse walk out of the line and trot back, then ask you to trot out and walk back. He's trying to see if you're paying attention.

Whenever you move your horse from a standstill to a walk in a showmanship class, *the horse should take the first step.* Just move your hand up and gracefully start him off, then after that first step, you begin.

Judges will often do something as tricky as laying over a section of the mane, as though checking for cleanliness underneath. Or, they'll move the top of the halter back, as though checking the bridle path. If anything like this is done, as soon as the judge is looking elsewhere, sneak up and move the halter back, or lay the mane back over and correct it. Do it so he doesn't see you do it.

Many showmanship exhibitors overdress and overshow. Even a contestant dressed in blue jeans and a long sleeved shirt looks sharp if everything is clean and fits well. Jackets and nice pants are definitely an asset, but not always necessary. The importance of the show should warrant how you dress. Don't dress for the Grand National, if you're showing in a small, backyard show.

Know the parts of the horse, what it is fed, and its age. Know what your number is. You'll never know what a showmanship judge is going to ask you during a class. When you reply, do it promptly and in an intelligent manner.

The biggest help you can have in showmanship classes is to watch several of them and try to memorize how the winners worked. When classes are done in an age breakdown, you'll often have a chance to watch the class before yours and, through concentration, you can spot the people who make even the slightest errors and can avoid making them yourself.

Remember that in a showmanship class you are being judged on your ability to fit and show a halter horse. You don't need a halter champion. You need a nicely fit horse, perfectly turned out to every detail, one that is wearing a well-fitted, clean halter, and is responding to it. And, when you show this horse, don't be a stiff machine—be a showman.

Wendy Daniels and Candy Bar . . . many times winners in showmanship.

When you're in the lineup, remember to stay out of the judge's sight. You can change sides of your horse by taking three small steps. On the third, you rotate and turn to face the head. If the judge is moving slowly around your horse, you will actually take three different positions. If he's on the right of your horse, you are on the left. As he goes behind the horse to look at the rear, you position yourself in front. As he goes to the left, you step to the right of the horse. The only exceptions to this are classes in Pinto and Appaloosa shows where a "Danger Zone" is described in the rule books, as these breed associations don't want handlers standing directly in front of the horses.

Attitude is extremely important in showmanship classes. While you remain serious and businesslike, you should never look sour or lose your polite appearance. If you feel the urge to scream because of trouble with your horse, hide the feeling until you're out of the ring.

Showmanship doesn't have to be nerveracking. It's an enjoyable class to show in. If you do your homework, then listen to the judge, there's no reason why you shouldn't win your share of classes!

Index

Absorbine, 76
American Paint Horse Association, 10–11
American Quarter Horse Association, 10
Amigo Babe, 5–6
Anderson, Al, 21, 61, 62, 192
Appaloosas, 13

Backing, 91–92
Balance, 22, 23, 28, 30
Ballard, John and Sandy, 18
Banding manes, 165
Bar Sprite, 88
Bathing, 118–119
Ben Bar, 49
Bitters, 100
Blanketing, 120–127
Boarding costs, 3
Body clipping, 152–154
Body suits, 126–127
Booting, 151–152
Boots, splint, 67, 81–83
Borden's foal lac, 36
Bottom line, bad, 101–102
Bradley, Stretch, 193
Braiding manes, 165
Breeding
    economics, 2–3
    for color, 10–14
    selecting mares and stallions, 3–9
    when to breed, 9–10
Bridle path, clipping, 143–145, 166–168
Bright Bars, 12, 14
Bright Chip, 13, 45, 88
Bright Coke Plaudit, 192
Bright Eyes, 12
Broodmares, 5–7, 9, 33–34
Bull rope, 63, 66
Bungee cords, 124
Burns, Dr. Jim, 4–10, 97, 101

Calf manna, 33, 34
California Livestock Symposium, 1
Campbell, Kenny, 79, 122, 195
Candy Bar, 211
Cannon bone, 27
Capay Miss Chips, 15

Care of feet and legs
    daily foot care, 74–78
    foot or hoof care, 72–73
    leg care, 68
    stocking up, 69
    wrapping legs, 69–72
Champion halter horses, 16–22
Chest, 28
Chestnuts, removing, 149–150
Class routine, 202
Classes, youth, 209–212
Clippers, 128, 130, 131, 153, 154
Clipping and trimming, 128, 129
    around the eyes, 137–138
    avoiding clipper marks, 152
    body clipping, 152–154
    bridle path, 143–145
    choosing restraints, 158–159
    earing down, 157–158
    ears, 138–143
    legs, 145–147, 151–152
    muzzles, 131–135
    removing ergots and chestnuts, 149–150
    restraining, 154–157
    shoulder hold, 158
    throatlatch, 135
    touch-up leg clipping, 147–148
    using clippers, 130–131
    when to clip, 130
Coats, 38–39
    coat care, 109–127
Coat oils, 38–39
Coat supplements, commercial, 38
Cohn, Joanie, 55, 112
Colic prevention, 41, 99
Colts, 28–30
Combing tails, 170–171
Come-along, 51, 66
Coy's Bonanza, 16
Creep feeding foals, 34–35
Cubes, 40

Daniels, Wendy, 211
Dart's Le Bar, 21
Department of Animal Science, USC, 1
Dia-glo, 38

Dressing the halter horse
  cleaning halters, 191–192
  halters, 177-186
  lead shank, 186–191
  silver halters, 193

Earing down, 157–158
Ears, clipping, 139–143
Ergots, 119, 149–150
Evans, Dr. Warren J., 1–3
Exercising halter horses, 79, 80, 81
  backing, 91–92
  free play, 88–89
  hill work, 94–95
  isometrics, 92–94
  longeing, 86–87
  ponying, 83–86
  riding, 95
  splint boots, 81–83
  treadmill, 89
  working both sides, 95
  working in the round pen, 89–91
Eyes, clipping around the, 137–138

Fabulous Farms, 45, 46
Feeding programs
  broodmares, 33–34
  colic prevention, 41
  creep feeding foals, 34–35
  feed management, 41
  hay, pellets, and cubes, 40
  mixing feeds, 32, 33
  three years and up, 38
  vitamins, 31, 35
  water and salt, 39–40
  weaning, 35–37
  working on the coat, 38–39
  yearlings and two-year-olds, 37–38
Feed costs, 3
Feed management, 41
Feet, brushing, 75–76
Feet, care of, 72–78
Flanigan, Burl, 29
Foals
  creep feeding, 34–35
  halter breaking, 45
  training weaned, 45–47
Foot size, 9
Forearm, 27
Forelocks, 166

Free play, 88–89
Fresno Livestock Symposium, 81

Gaskins, 24, 29, 30
Glisteners, 168
Gonigan, John, 21
Grass, 100
Grooming, 109, 111–117
  bathing, 118–119
  blanketing, 120–127
Gullets, 179, 180

Halcyon Farms, 13, 14, 45, 46, 90
Halter breaking foals, 45
Halter horse
  breeding, 1–15
  care of feet and legs, 67–78
  clipping and trimming, 128–159
  coat care and grooming, 109–127
  dressing, 177–193
  exercise, 79–95
  feeding and worming programs, 31–43
  manes and tails, 160–176
  selecting a halter prospect, 17–30
  showing, 194–212
  training, 44-66
  working on problem areas, 96–108
  young, 28–30
Halter horses, judging, 22–28
Halter prospects, selecting, 17–30
Halters, 177–181
  adjusting, 181
  cleaning, 191–192
  matching halter to head, 181–186
  silver, 193
Hay, 40
Head, 23
Heart girth, 24
Hereditary traits, 7
Hill work, 94–95
Hip, 24
Hocks, 24
Hoods, 123–124
Hoof black, 196, 199, 200
Hoof care, 72–78
Hoof dressings, 74
"Horse raincoats," 125
Hug N Tuff, 112, 139

Isometrics, 92–94

Judging foals, 28–30
Judging halter horses, 202–207, 209–212
  back legs, 25, 27
  balance, 22, 23, 24
  cannon bone, 27
  chest, 28
  foals, 28–30
  forearm, 27
  front legs, 27
  gaskins, 24, 26, 29, 30
  head, 23
  heart girth, 24
  hip, 24
  hocks, 24
  neck, 23
  plumb line, 27
  posterns, 27, 28
  shoulders, 23, 27
  splints, 28
  throatlatch, 23
  traveling, 28
  withers, 23, 24

Kane, Tim, 80, 89, 114
Koppertox, 74

Leading out, 48–51
Lead shank, 62, 63, 64, 186–191
Legs, clipping, 145–147
  avoiding clipper marks, 152
  booting, 151–152
  touch-up clipping, 147–148
Legs, back, 25, 27
Legs, care of, 68–72
Legs, front, 27
Legs, wrapping, 68, 69–72
"Leo" line, 11, 12
Leo Tag, 11
Lip cord, 156
Lixotinic, 99
Long, Tom and Brenda, 86–87
Longeing, 86–87

Manes, 160
  adding glisteners, 168
  braiding, weighting, banding, 165
  bridle path, 166–168
  conditioning, 166
  foretop, 166
  length, 165–166
  rubbed out mane, 168
  thinning, 161–165
Manion, Tommy, 81, 109
Muscle definition, improving, 107–108
Mutton withers, 107
Muzzles, clipping, 131–135

Neck, 23
  neck sweats, 79, 103, 104, 167
  neck wraps, 102, 103, 106
  trimming, 102
Neff, Dukem, 6

Obesity, 97–98
Oils, coat, 38–39
Omalene, 32, 33, 35
Orvus, 118

Paint Breeding Stock Registry, 12
Paints, 10–12
Parasite control, 41–43
Parrot mouth, 7
Paul F. Bar, 18
Pellets, 40
Plumb line, 27
Ponying, 83–86
Posterns, 27, 28
Potter, Dr. Gary, 41
Preparation for showing, 194–201
Problem areas, working on, 96
  bad bottom line, 101–102
  improving muscle definition, 107–108
  mutton withers, 107
  obesity, 97–98
  trimming the neck, 102–107
  underweight horse, 98–101
Prostaglandin, 10
Purina Big 'Un, 32, 35
Purina Horse Charge, 33, 34
Purina Omalene, 32, 35

Reducine, 76
Restraints, 154–159
Ricky Bonanza, 16, 17
Riding, 95
Ring, handling trouble in the, 207–209
Rope, bull, 63, 66
Robin Reed, 13, 14
Rodeo Cowboy, 11, 36, 92
Rooster Cogburn, 121
Round pen, working in the, 89–91

Routine, class, 202
Rubbed out manes, 168

Sanitary conditions, 43
Scamp's Patches, 97
Sea kelp, 38
Shampoos, 118
Shank, chain, 62, 63, 64
Sharp, Eugene and Doris, 13, 45, 46, 84
Shoeing, 72–73
Shoulder, 23
Showing halter horses, 194
  handling trouble in the ring, 207–209
  learning class routine, 202
  preparation, 194–201
  walking in individually, 202–205
  walking to judge, turning, trotting, 205–207
  youth showmanship, 209–212
Skipa Star, 16, 17
Skipper's Lad, 16
Skipper W., 16
Silva, Paul, 29
Soybean meal, 38
Splint boots, 67, 81–83
Splints, 28
Stage Hand, 12
Stage W., 12
Stallions, dressing, 185, 186
Standing still, 58–61
Standing square, 61–62
  off the halter, 62–66
Stickler, Harry, 45, 48, 51, 52, 53
Stickler, Lynn, 45, 47
"Stocking up," 69
Stopping, 56–58
Sugar Wes, 18, 19, 20, 21

Tails, 160, 168–170
  combing, 170–171
  helping tail to grow, 173
  protecting from sun and wind, 173
  thinning, 171–173
  wrapping, 173–176

Throatlatch, 23, 85, 106, 107
  clipping, 135
  wraps, 102, 103, 104, 105
Thyrone, 98
Tight turns, 52–56
Top Yellow, 12
Training halter horses
  foals, 44–45
  leading out, 48–51
  standing still, 58–61
  standing square, 61–66
  teaching tight turns, 52–56
  the stop, 56–58
  weaned foals, 45–47
Traits, hereditary, 7
Treadmill, 89
Trimming, *see* clipping and trimming
Turns, tight, 52–56
Twitches, 156–157
2J Horse Farm, 10, 12
Two-year-olds, 37–38
Tyznik, Dr. William J., 37, 38

Underweight horses, 98–101

Vet costs, 3
Vetrap, 68, 70, 71, 196
Vitamins, 31, 35, 78

Walking, 202–207
Weaning, 35–37
Weighting manes, 165
Wells, Jerry, 110
Wendy Ann Wes, 20
Williamson, Joe, 12
Williamson, Stanley, 10
Wilson Ranch, 16
Windy Hill Ranch, 18
Withers, 23, 24
  mutton, 107
Worming programs, 98–99
  parasite control, 41–43
  sanitary conditions, 43
Wrapping tails, 173, 176

Yearlings, 37–38
Yellow Mount, 12
Youth classes, 209–212